Cockatiels as a Hobby

Jack C. Harris

SAVE-OUR-PLANET SERIES

Contents

Distributed in the UNITED STATES by T.F.H. Publications, Inc., One T.F.H. Plaza, Neptune City, NJ 07753; in CANADA to the Pet Trade by H & L Pet Supplies Inc., 27 Kingston Crescent, Kitchener, Ontario N2B 2T6; Rolf C. Hagen Ltd., 3225 Sartelon Street, Montreal 382 Quebec; in CANADA to the Book Trade by Macmillan of Canada (A Division of Canada Publishing Corporation), 164 Commander Boulevard, Agincourt, Ontario M1S 3C7; in ENGLAND by T.F.H. Publications, PO Box 15, Waterlooville PO7 6BQ; in AUSTRALIA AND THE SOUTH PACIFIC by T.F.H. (Australia) Pty. Ltd., Box 149, Brookvale 2100 N.S.W., Australia; in NEW ZEALAND by Ross Haines & Son, Ltd., 82 D Elizabeth Knox Place, Panmure, Auckland, New Zealand; in the PHILIPPINES by Bio-Research, 5 ... age, Makati, Rizal; in SOUTH ...). Box 35347, Northway, 4065, ... Publications, Inc. Manufactured ... y T.F.H. Publications, Inc.

Introduction

A pet is described in the dictionary as "A tame animal treated lovingly or kept as a companion: any loved and cherished creature or thing." While this definition can be aptly applied to any pet, it appears to be most especially applicable to the cockatiel. These exotic and beautiful birds are easy to train, clean, and house, and offer years of enjoyable and exciting fun. They can be taught to speak a few words and are relatively easy to breed in captivity, even for a beginner. This reputation has earned them a solid second place behind the more common budgerigar, as the most popular pet bird. All of its characteristics, both unique and common, make it the very essence of "pet."

Regardless of the kind of pet you're choosing, the more you know about its care and feeding, the better. Caring for a pet is a great responsibility for anyone, no matter how "easy" that care is reputed to be. Beyond learning the basics of care and handling, finding out about the natural history of your animal will add an extra dimension to the joys of owning a pet. If you know where your pet's ancestors came from and how the animal was originally

Opposite: The cockatiel as an art form? This artfully posed photo shows a beautiful melding of natural forms. Photo by Michael Gilroy.

Above: A bird on the hand is worth two in the bush; the ultimate of hand-taming a cockatiel! Photo by N. Richmond.

domesticated and trained, you will better appreciate the problems and satisfactions to be faced as the caretaker of a new pet.

This volume was written to introduce you to the cockatiel. We will examine the bird's origins, its discovery, and the current and recognized theories on care, feeding, housing, training, and breeding of these colorful creatures. If you have already decided to acquire a cockatiel as a pet, this will serve as your guidebook. If you are examining this book to learn about the birds in order to actually make a final decision about owning one, then we will aid you in making up your mind.

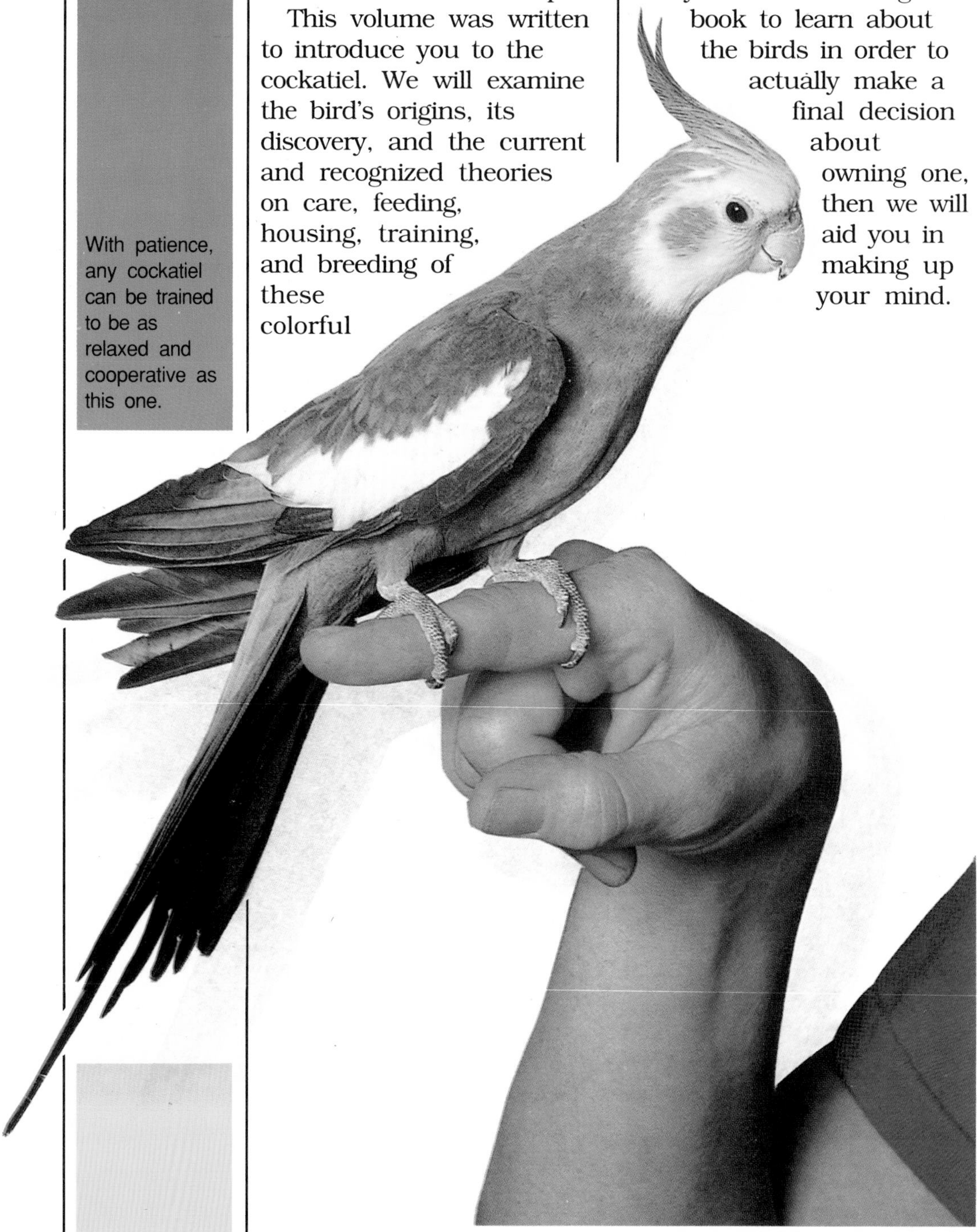

With patience, any cockatiel can be trained to be as relaxed and cooperative as this one.

What is a Cockatiel?

A normal gray (left) and gray pied cockatiel taking their ease. Photo by Michael Gilroy.

Scientifically, the Cockatiel is classified as *Nymphicus hollandicus.* It belongs to the order Psittaciformes, which birds are commonly called parrots. There is, however, some controversy regarding the exact classification. While many experts consider the bird as part of the parrot subfamily, others contend that it is a miniature cockatoo. The specific differences that various experts have put forth seem to indicate that the cockatiel lies somewhere *between* the parrot and cockatoo subfamilies, enjoying habits and characteristics of both. We will not be joining in the controversy in this publication. The bird owners themselves can make up their own minds after they get to know their new pets.

Cockatiels are native to

Australia, normally being found almost everywhere in that country except for the coastal regions. In the wild they are found in small groups in dense forests, lowlands, and even desert regions with low-growing vegetation. They are nomadic birds, seeking areas where the food and water supply is easily accessible. For this reason there are often large flocks of them seen in areas where none have been previously reported. In the southern sections of the country, the cockatiels' movements appear to be migratory in nature, arriving in the area during the first weeks of spring. They will remain there for breeding and then begin a return migration north.

PHYSICAL CHARACTERISTICS

The cockatiel is recognized by its distinctive head coloring. The adult cocks have bright yellow heads, with a white patch in the middle and a long, tapering, yellow crest. The most striking features are the bright fire-orange cheek patches directly under its ebony-or brown-irised eyes. The upper-tail coverts and rump are colored silver-gray and the under-tail coverts are so dark that they often run to black. The beak and feet are gray in color as well. The adult male appears stockier than a juvenile and usually displays a crest

In the wild, cockatiels use dead trees and other natural cavities as nesting sites. Photo by Dr. Gerald R. Allen.

that is slightly depressed.

As is the case in most of nature (although not always the case in the parrot family), the hens are not as brightly colored as the cocks. However, with cockatiels, the differences are not entirely obvious, and close examination is needed to determine the sex of different birds. Generally, the hens have more gray on the heads and yellow bands on the underside of the tail. The females are sometimes noted by additional yellow coloring around their eyes, their foreheads, and on the lower section of their throats. Yellow spots are also evident on the hens' wings. These color identifications are widely varied since there is much selective breeding specifically for color in cockatiels.

The juvenile cockatiels are very similar to the hens and usually cannot be sexually identified until they are at least six months of age. The cocks, at this age, will usually develop the yellow head coloring, but the full process is not complete until adulthood at about one year old. The juveniles' crests are almost constantly erect. Younger birds also have lighter beaks and their feathers are softer than those of adults. Their feet appear more pink than the gray feet of older birds. At the age of approximately three months, a young cockatiel's beak will grow dark after going through a brownish stage. Their beaks appear pink at birth.

Adult cockatiels usually measure from 10 to 13

These two splendid specimens, a cinnamon (left) and pearl (right), illustrate the variety possible in the selective breeding of cockatiels. Photo by H. Bielfeld.

inches long from the top of the crest to the tip of the tail. They have a life span of 15 to 25 years.

In their natural habitat, they have been observed feeding on such available food as the seeds of various native grasses, herb-like shrubs, plants, trees, berries, grain, fruit, acacia seeds, mistletoe berries, millet, etc. They feed on the ground rather than in the trees, utilizing their natural coloring for camouflage.

The aborigines of Australia have long hunted the birds for food and enjoy the birds' eggs as well. The first European reports of the cockatiel came from

The wild colors of the cockatiel (right) are no less attractive than the cultivated pied strain, shown at left. Photo by Michael Gilroy.

the naturalists who joined Captain James Cook as he voyaged near Australia's east coast in 1770. Specimens from this and other voyages were never documented with complete scientific accuracy, but later descriptions of them from the archives of the Royal College of Surgeons in England seem to indicate that some were indeed the cockatiels that we know today. In the latter part of the 18th century, the scientist Gmelin spoke of the "wedge-tailed cockatoo" and the "cockatoo parakeet" in his work entitled *Systema Naturae.* His references are due to the cockatiel's strong resemblance to the cockatoo.

Although not completely documented, the first successful breeding

The golden lutino is about as dramatic a departure from the original wild cockatiel as one can get! Photo by N. Richmond.

The conspicuous white wing patch of the wild cockatiel is retained in all but the palest of the cultivated strains. Photo by Isabelle Francais.

of cockatiels in captivity was achieved in Germany in the middle of the 19th century. The London Zoo reported such success in 1863 after de tailed reports on breeding the birds were published by Leuckfeld in 1858. These even helped the birds become well-known favorites in various zoological gardens and private aviaries around the world.

It wasn't until 1839 that European reports of cockatiels in the wild were published. These came from John Gould, the famous British naturalist, who noted large flocks of the birds in eastern Australia. He observed many other now commonly known characteristics of the birds, including their flight patterns, procurement of food, and breeding habits.

The cockatiel speeds along in a straight line and lands by letting itself fall straight down, stopping its descent with outspread wings just prior to hitting the ground.

BEHAVIOR IN THE WILD

The cockatiel's natural enemies include

small and medium-sized birds of prey that swoop down on the unwary, especially during feeding time. Because of the low-growing native vegetation and the fact that they feed almost exclusively on the ground, their enemies can easily strike a flock of hungry cockatiels. The birds' natural fear manifests itself when they are on the ground by causing them to immediately take to the air at even the slightest disturbance. Often, whatever has startled a flock is undetectable by human observers. All may appear calm and peaceful, but then, seemingly for no reason, a flock of cockatiels in the wild will take to the air as one, perching at the highest possible observation point.

This fear is also quite evident when they visit the local water hole. They will circle high above for long periods of time, searching for possible enemies before swooping down into the water for a few sips in as many seconds. They are then back in the air again. They are never seen landing on the shore and casually taking a sip. Since they often inhabit arid areas, they are able to sustain themselves for long periods on very little water intake.

A solitary cockatiel would be an unusual sight in Australia; the birds there assemble in flocks numbering in the thousands. Photo by T. Tilford.

Instinctively, the birds seem to be aware of the power of their natural camouflage. When they are perched on the dead branches of shrubs or trees, it is often possible to approach them quite closely before they fly away. They enhance their coloring by assuming positions similar to the surrounding foliage. When the effect is fully accomplished, it is often extremely difficult to notice that the birds are even there.

Cockatiels, once they have chosen a mate for breeding, will remain as an individual pair throughout the entire year, even after the normal breeding season is over. They usually seek out existing holes about five to ten inches across and 15 to 30 inches deep in dead trees. They choose a location that is about six feet off the ground and one that offers unobstructed views 360 degrees around. They do not alter these existing holes, preferring the natural state. It is difficult, therefore, to give a general, overall description of a cockatiel nest.

While they prefer dead trees, they will nest in living trees as well. In larger nesting trees, cockatiels have been seen sharing the other branches with others of their own kind and cockatoos in additional nesting holes.

The cockatiel breeding season is totally dependent upon the various rainy seasons in Australia. This occurs in the Australian spring months, from August to December in the southern regions. The cockatiels observed in the northern areas of the country appear to prefer the latter part of the rainy season for their breeding, around April to June. The conditions caused by the weather provide the ample food supply that the birds instinctively realize will be needed for feeding their young. New shoots are sprouting, flowers are blooming, and seeds are in

A view of cockatiels in their "natural" habitat—a telephone wire along an Australian road.

abundance. The conditions in the central regions of the country allow the cockatiels to breed whenever the general conditions are ideal, after a rainy period.

As a general rule, a pair of breeding cockatiels will produce a single nest each year. Two have been reported when there has been more than the usual amount of rainfall, assuring an ongoing food supply. A courting pair of cockatiels will be seen grooming one another, cooing, kissing, snuggling, and even feeding each other. They will sing to each other and appear to thoroughly enjoy being together. They might have little disagreements, but they will soon return to preening each other and their pair-bonding rituals will continue. They are almost inseparable. They will also spend a great deal of time exploring the immediate area of the nest. This is probably due to their instinctive need to protect one another and the coming young.

Other birds display quite a bit of elaborate and unusual behavior during these times, but such is not the general case with cockatiels. Male cockatiels have been seen, on many

Above and Left: Cockatiels quartered in large aviaries readily utilize any tree cavities as nest sites, as this captive pair has. Photos by Dr. Gerald R. Allen.

occasions, displaying a subtle pre-mating ritual of lifting their shoulders, holding their wings out with the tops remaining across the back, holding their heads high and repeating the melodic cockatiel call.

Copulatory periods vary widely but are usually anywhere from one to ten minutes, and several may take place during any 24-hour period. When the hen is prepared for mating, she will lower her back, making it appear flat. The male will mount and stand on her back, sometimes using its claws to secure itself. The position is quite similar to that observed in mammals. After the cock has mounted, the hen lifts her wing and the male begins swinging his tail to the side and under her until their vents meet. The female often makes quiet squeaking

Mutual grooming and displays of affection are common behavioral traits among all parrots, especially so the cockatiel.

If you must handle a fledgling cockatiel, do so with care. This breeder is preventing the chick from bolting by gently holding its tail feathers.

noises, and the male will sometimes sing with the familiar cockatiel call. More often than not, the male is silent, frequently opening and closing his beak. The male's testes excrete sperm into the cloaca through the sperm duct and it is then passed up the oviduct to the ovum, where fertilization takes place. The egg forms quickly, within only a few days from copulation to egg laying.

A cockatiel clutch usually numbers four to five eggs. If the food supply has been better than average, there may be six or seven eggs in the clutch. The eggs are ivory colored and about the size of an almond. Both the hen and the cock will take their turns sitting on the eggs during the incubation period. This is a common trait with cockatoos. The hen will sit on them during the night while the cock stands guard near the entrance to the nest hollow. The cock takes his turn incubating the eggs during the day. The birds will remain very close to the nest during the entire incubation period, never straying far even for feeding. The cock will spend the majority of his time, when not sitting on the eggs, perched near the nesting hollow entrance. After about 18 to 21 days, the chicks will hatch. The eggs hatch in the order in which they were originally laid, usually one chick hatching every two days. A fluffy coat of bright yellow down covers newly hatched cockatiels. Their eyes are closed at hatching, but will normally open within a week to ten days. The cockatiel parents will care for and feed the offspring for about a four- or five-week period until the young are old enough to finally leave the nesting hollow. Young birds will

The grace and beauty of the cockatiel. especially in some of the colorful cultivated strains, has made it one of the world's most popular pets. Photo by Michael Gilroy.

crouch on a perch and loudly shriek as a signal to their parents that it is time to regurgitate their food and feed the young. After about two weeks, the young will start to feed on their own. The parents will continue to feed the young birds for a few weeks after this until the new cockatiels become fully independent. The mother and father share the feeding duties, partially ingesting food for the young and feeding it to them mouth to mouth, holding it first in the crop, part of the bird's esophagus. The female usually does most of the feeding, but generally the chore is shared.

The well-documented habits of cockatiels in the wild and the long years of observation in captivity have helped to illustrate how ideally suited the birds are for pets. They adapt well in captivity and exist happily in relatively small cages as well as larger private aviaries. Over their years in captivity, the birds have attained a highly developed sense of play. They can be taught to speak a few simple words and sometimes to repeat tunes they have heard. This fact and their natural and selectively bred beauty have made them sought-after as pets throughout the world.

Choosing Your Cockatiel

While the cockatiel population in Australia is enormous, there is a complete and total ban on exporting the birds. In most areas of the United States, the birds can be purchased at a local pet shop. The supply is normally adequate, but at certain times of the year, there may be a shortage due to high demand or other unforeseen circumstances. Pet shops are usually happy to place on a waiting list the names of eager, potential Cockatiel owners so they will be able to have their bird as soon as the stock is back to acceptable levels.

Since they are the experts, pet shop owners strive to keep their stock in excellent health.

The wise cockatiel buyer will spend some time interacting with his or her prospective pet before deciding to purchase.

cockatiels are extremely adaptable birds and remain hale and hardy for the most part. If a bird *is* suffering from an illness, the pet shop owner will not be offering it for sale until it has regained its health. Nevertheless, it is always a good policy to personally, carefully observe and also closely examine any pet in its pet shop environment prior to making a purchase.

Cockatiels enjoy a reputation for being sociable birds. However, like most birds and small animals, they are easily startled. When examining your potential pet for the first time, be sure that it can see you coming. Don't sneak up on it. Approach slowly; and do not make any sudden movements or loud noises. Talking softly and whistling are reassurance techniques used in training and taming cockatiels. It is noted here since speaking softly to the birds as you come close to

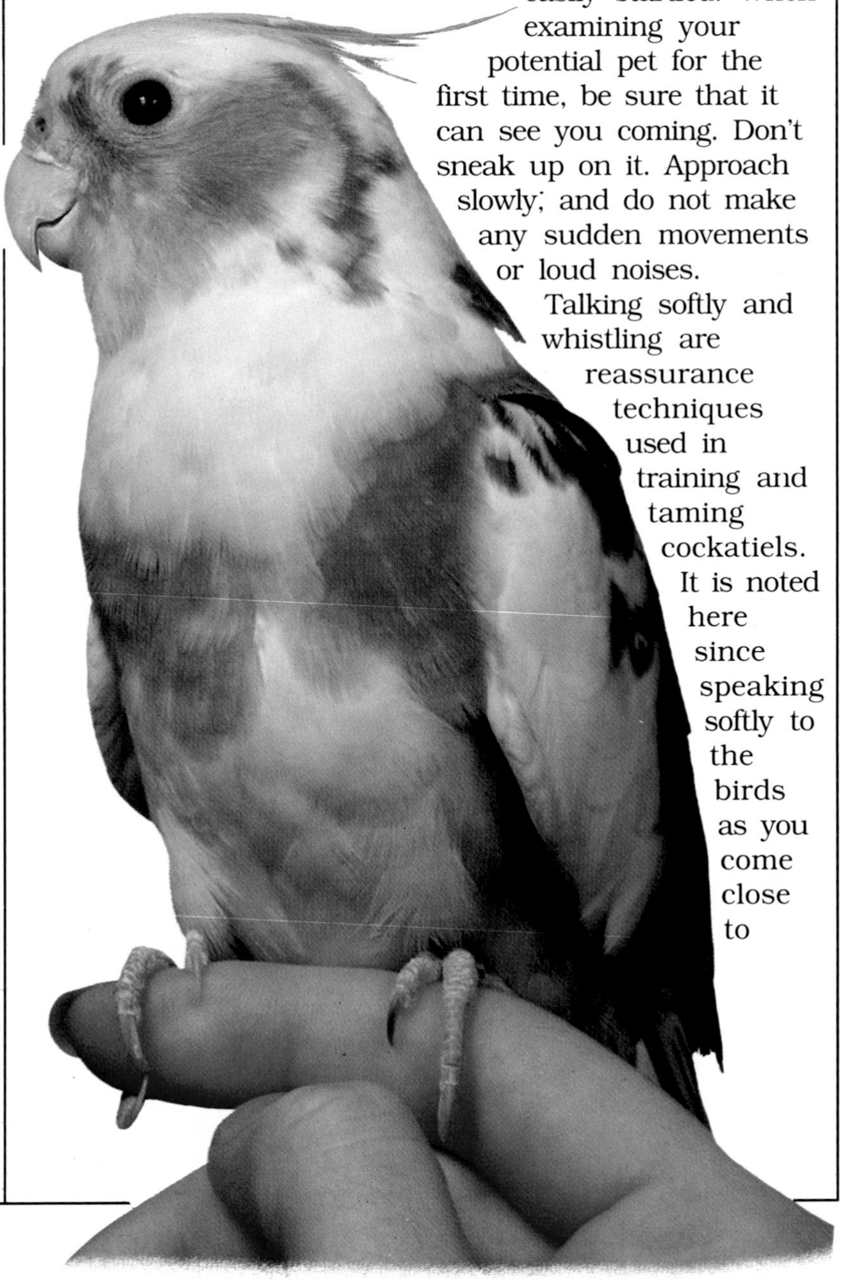

This finger-tamed cockatiel shows the clean plumage and clear, bright eye of the the healthy cockatiel. Photo by Michael Gilroy.

them for the first time and whistling while you observe them at close hand helps to calm them. If the bird is upset or startled, you will not get an accurate representation of its personality and reactions towards human beings.

WHAT TO LOOK FOR IN A COCKATIEL

Watching a particular bird's activities for about half an hour should give you enough superficial information to determine its general health. If the bird you like spends long periods of time sitting still on its perch, or if it is in any way lethargic, there are probably health problems. A healthy cockatiel will be pretty active and be seen preening, eating, and otherwise enjoying itself. If the contrary appears to be the case, take a closer look at the cockatiel's feathers. The plumage should be sleek and smooth and lie close to the bird's body, not fluffed out. The bird should sit proud and upright on its perch. If you see it keeping its head tucked in its wings, it is most likely not feeling well.

Examine the animal's eyes. One with clear eyes is normally healthy. If the eyes appear puffy, watery, or glassy, this is a fairly reliable indication that sickness is either present or about to overtake the bird. If the bird suffers from a runny nose, or if loose droppings are seen in its cage, choose another cockatiel. Take a look at the bird's claws and feet too. If there are any abnormalities present, that particular bird is probably not the one to choose.

Most first-time owners want to purchase a younger bird for several reasons. First of all, they have a potentially longer time to enjoy the bird as a pet if it is purchased as a nestling. Secondly, younger birds are easier to train since they have had less time to be trained by others or to become set in their ways.

There are some cockatiel experts who feel that the birds should be purchased only in pairs; however, an equally large number of cockatiel connoisseurs feel there will be no problems

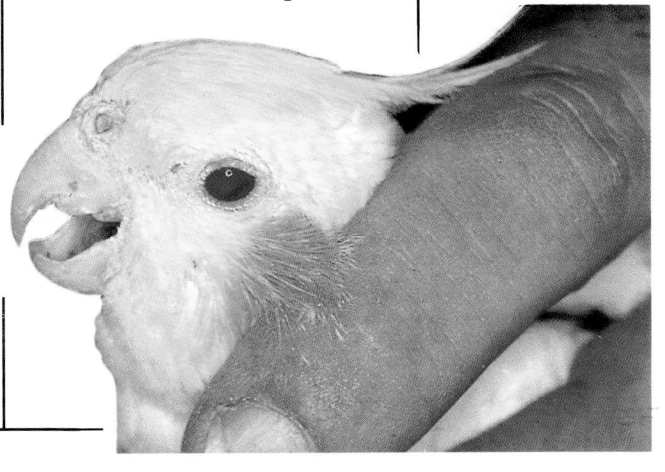

The cockatiel is a nut and seed eater, but its sharp, powerful bill can deliver a nasty bite if a bird is handled roughly. Photo by Michael Gilroy.

The pale bill and slim profile of this bird indicate that it is fairly young. Photo by Michael Gilroy.

in raising and training a single bird. In fact, many of this latter group believe that the single Cockatiel will prove to be a better pet.

If the age of your potential pet cockatiel is a consideration, your local pet shop owner will help you determine the approximate age of whatever bird you have your eye on. In some cases, if the pet shop owner is also a breeder, he will most likely have a complete record of the bird's birth and medical history. If not, he will probably have some older adult birds by which you can make comparisons of size, coloring, proportion, etc. Cockatiels tend to become stockier as they grow older, so younger birds actually appear to be more slender than their parents. When hatched and for about three months afterwards, the birds' bills are pink, turning to gray thereafter. This is another way to get an estimate of a bird's approximate age.

Also, the eyes of younger, nestling birds still are entirely black and have light iridial rings. In the case of the standard gray-colored cockatiels, some males may be more easily identified because the bright yellow head plumage appears sooner. However, this is not a completely accurate sexing technique. Also, personality traits, even in these young birds, should have a determining factor in selecting the one you wish for a companion. If the bird appears somewhat shy, it may have more potential as a pet since the bolder birds obviously have become more independent and would be more resistant to training.

Equal success has been noted in training males and females. There is no discernible difficulty in taming either sex or in teaching them to talk. Both cocks and hens make excellent pets.

Some people may be looking for an older bird that has already been trained. Your pet shop dealer may be able to refer you to someone in this regard. However, the cautions regarding the examination of the bird you are about to buy are even more crucial in cases such as these than if you're buying from a pet shop. Pet shops often guarantee the health of their animals and will exchange them if the customer is not satisfied. Private sellers offering such a guarantee are few and far between. Before you make *any* purchase of a pet, from a store or an individual pet owner, be certain you understand their guarantees and what they cover, and their policies regarding the health, return, or exchange of the pet. Prices of the birds vary widely

Cockatiels, like most psittacine birds, will chew on and demolish wood objects placed in their quarters. Photo by Isabelle Francais.

Pet cockatiels can be allowed to fly free in a home—but under supervision!

around the world due to common economic factors as well as the rarity of certain color variations of particular cockatiels and simple supply and

demand. Potential pet owners are urged to shop wisely, taking price variations into consideration right alongside the health and personality traits of the birds they are observing. All of these factors must be weighed by the careful pet shopper. Regarding color, the most common type of cockatiel is the "wild colored" birds. These are predominantly gray, the normal color of the majority of the birds in their native Australian homeland. Since they have been in captivity, selective breeding has, of course, produced a range of mutated color varieties. The rarity of certain colors, some of which include white, yellow, cinnamon, etc., often have a determining factor in pricing. Again, different color varieties and their availability vary from area to area. Selective shopping is still the answer to finding the most reasonable price for the kind of pet bird you wish to own.

There are certain other factors which should be taken into consideration if you are selecting cockatiels for breeding purposes which we will be detailing later.

Housing Your Cockatiel

The purchase of any pet is never a singular thing. Along with the animal itself you must be prepared to buy the accessories that the pet will need to survive in your home. In the case of cockatiels, the major accessory purchase will be its cage.

Since there are entirely different considerations to make if you have more than one bird or if you are buying birds as pets or for breeding, we will assume, at first, that you have decided on a single cockatiel as a pet.

IMPORTANT CONSIDERATIONS

Two important things you must keep in mind are style of cage and its eventual location in your home. Although they have been in captivity for many generations, cockatiels are still creatures of the outdoors. They still enjoy and need the wide open spaces. They will adapt well to captivity, but they do require their space. Selection and positioning of a cage is of primary importance to your cockatiel's future well-being.

This cage, while adequate for the two lovebirds shown here, would only be suitable for a single cockatiel. Photo by Isabelle Francais.

Cages for cockatiels should be roomy. The recognized standard-sized cage for the larger variety of parrots is usually an excellent choice, as well as those cages made for the bigger parakeets. The smaller the cage, the more daily exercise your bird will need flying, supervised, outside of its cage. No matter how large these individual bird cages are, if confined in one, cockatiels still have to have the

Stripped tree branches placed in the cage or aviary will offer your cockatiels plenty of chewing exercise.

opportunity to stretch their wings. These flying sessions should be closely supervised since cockatiels have been known to cause considerable damage with their strong beaks and claws.

The perfect cockatiel cage should be of all-metal construction. These are much easier to keep clean, and they are sturdy enough to withstand the bird's chewing instinct. Ease of cleaning is further facilitated by a cage that has a plastic, drawer-like, pull-out bottom. These should be covered with ordinary newspapers or commercial cage-bottom coverings. Some of these coverings come with fine gravel or sand already adhered. If not, it's best to sprinkle some evenly to help absorb droppings. Since cockatiels are very clean birds, it should not be necessary to clean the cage bottom every day. About three times a week, all you need do is remove the bottom covering and replace it with a fresh one. If you detect, however, that your bird has developed mites, you should clean the entire cage in a large tub of water with a household germicide, scrubbing it clean with a wire brush. Be sure that it is perfectly dry before returning the bird to its cage.

The cage should measure at least two feet in all directions, allowing your cockatiel to fly inside it without having to fear bumping its wings or tail into metal wires during every flight.

At least two sides of any cage you select should have horizontal bars.

Cockatiels enjoy climbing, and this would be impossible for them to accomplish with all vertical bars since those provide no secure footholds. There is also a danger presented if there are no horizontal bars since the birds will try to climb regardless of the direction of the bar.

The birds may put their heads between vertical bars and, not being able to support themselves, they could strangle.

Natural wood perches have a more pleasing appearance and provide a source of vitamins through the wood. Photo by Horst Bielfeld.

PERCHES

Most cages come with a perch or perches already installed. Many experts highly recommend replacing these perches with those of natural wood about three-quarters inch in diameter from freshly cut hazel nut, willow or fruit trees. Be certain that the wood you use is from trees that have not been treated with any chemicals. Since the birds enjoy chewing so much, the wood beneath the bark of these branches will provide vitamins for them. The uneven nature of these fresh branches will also help to exercise the bird's feet. These natural branches will have to be replaced every so often as they will be worn down by the bird's activity.

This sturdy galvanized metal feed tray is typical of the practical cage utensil. Photo by Dr. Gerald Allen.

FEEDING UTENSILS

The majority of the cages you can purchase in your local pet store come already equipped with containers for water and seeds. You may have to make substitutions for the specific needs of your cockatiel since these birds are ground feeders. Seed can be placed in heavy porcelain or earthenware containers on the floor of the cage, provided they are not directly beneath the perches. Proper placement of these containers will prevent contamination from the bird's droppings. The heavy containers will not be tipped over by the bird's activity.

BATHS

Normal rainfall in the wild will give the cockatiels most of the "bath" time they desire, although some have been seen splashing at the edges of streams. Cockatiels have a gland at the base of their tails that many of the birds in captivity have been seen using to groom their feathers while preening. Some pet birds don't like water at all. However, others enjoy a bath, so it is a good idea to

A clay flowerpot saucer makes an ideal, non-tippable bathing dish. Photo by Dr. Gerald R. Allen.

provide a shallow, non-tippable dish filled with fresh water. Never use any sort of shampoo or soap in the bath dish.

The bath can be placed in the cage for about half an hour every few days. Cockatiels usually get only their feet and underbelly wet. Some birds prefer to bathe only when they are free from their cage. The dish can be placed outside the cage during flying time, and the bird will seek it out if desired. Some pet owners fill a sink with a shallow depth of water if one is available in the room that houses the cockatiel.

Other cockatiels enjoy being sprayed with water from a garden hose or an atomizer when their cages are hung out-of-doors for an airing. Try each method a few times and then stick to the one that your bird seems to prefer.

TOYS

Just as parakeets do, cockatiels enjoy a variety of bird toys, which can also be found at your local pet shop. Mirrors, small bells, swinging ladders, etc., are all favorites of the cockatiel. Make certain that they are constructed of wood or materials that are non-toxic and unbreakable. The cockatiel's energetic activity and chewing habits could lead to disaster for your pet otherwise.

Resist the temptation to fill the cage with all kinds of exotic perches and bird toys. Too many of such things will only take up more of the already limited flying space the bird requires.

SITING THE CAGE

Also of extreme importance is the location of your pet cockatiel's cage in your home. Cockatiels need a light room that is free from drafts and is well-ventilated. Make certain they are not exposed to direct, strong sunlight for

Most cockatiel and parrot cage toys serve two functions: play and exercise through chewing activity. Photos by Isabelle Francais.

The pet cockatiel soon comes to recognize its cage as "home base" and will return to it when allowed to fly free. Photo by Horst Bielfeld.

any extended periods of time. If there is a room that the potential owner enjoys spending long hours in comfortably, then this is probably an ideal spot for a cockatiel cage.

Over the generations of being in captivity, many cockatiels have developed a coat of down feathers that is not as thick and protective as that of their brothers in the wild. This is why the cage location should be away from any drafts. A cockatiel trapped in an extended draft could easily catch a cold and possibly die.

In the wild, cockatiels have been found living comfortably in areas with temperatures ranging from 40° F. to 110° F. in the shade. Those kept in captivity thrive best in temperatures between 40 F. and 50 F. during the night and anywhere from 65° F. to 80° F. during the daylight hours. Avoid subjecting your pet to sudden temperature fluctuations.

Cockatiels like to be sociable, so don't put their cage off in some lonely room where they do not have the chance to interact with people on a regular basis. With this in mind, also be sure that the cage is situated in such a way that they can see people approaching. They can be easily startled, so you should avoid placing the cage next to a door where people can enter the room suddenly. Such approaches could distress your pet. While many bird keepers cover their birds' cages at night, this is really not necessary in the case of the cockatiel. They enjoy seeing the goings-on in the surrounding room as well as the return of daylight in the early morning. If you're planning a party where your cockatiel's room will be filled with a large group, it also might be a good suggestion to cover the

As cockatiels are highly sociable birds, they should either get plenty of human attention or be kept in pairs. An ignored, single cockatiel is a very unhappy one! Photo by N. Richmond.

cage or, if possible, remove it completely to a location with less commotion.

Many pet owners bring their birds outside in their cages for a few hours each day during the warmer months. If such is your desire, be sure that there are no other pets such as dogs or cats in the vicinity, which could frighten your bird. If other animals are present, you may want to suspend the bird's cage from a tree or a clothesline. Also, be certain that the cage bottom and doors are securely fastened during these outings. Even if the bird's wings have been clipped, there is danger of escape.

Some of the handier cockatiel owners who have the space have elected to construct an indoor aviary for their birds. This is usually not done for a single bird, since single cockatiels can thrive in a smaller cage. However, if the space is available and the pet owner is inclined to construct one, an indoor aviary is a joy for any cockatiel to inhabit. A garage, a shed, or an attic are all excellent locations for an indoor aviary as long as the same conditions are present as those required for the smaller indoor cages. The aviary should be light, spacious, away from drafts and not subject to any drastic fluctuation of normal temperature.

Aviaries are available commercially in many handsome designs, but a perfectly suitable indoor aviary can be made by a handy pet owner with simple materials available at most local hardware or "do-it-yourself" stores. Wire mesh and wood are the basic materials, remembering again that food containers must be kept away from perches. Most indoor aviaries have a special shelf for food located about halfway between the floor and the ceiling.

Cleaning such an aviary might be a larger task since most

indoor aviaries utilize the room's floor itself. It should be swept out whenever necessary. Normally, a pet owner constructs a low doorway for access to an indoor aviary.

THE OUTDOOR AVIARY

For breeding purposes, many bird owners construct an outdoor aviary. The knowledgeable do-it-yourself pet owner can construct one of these on his own, and the novice with the space and capital can hire a patio or similar contracting firm to construct such an accommodation. In either case, an aviary of even adequate size will probably be large enough to require a local building permit. Along with some additional structures and necessities, most of the same requirements for all the aforementioned accommodations are necessary for outdoor aviaries, but they have added importance because of the larger scale.

Also, since a flock of cockatiels can be extremely noisy, it may be necessary to obtain special permits depending on the zoning of your particular neighborhood. If your neighbors themselves

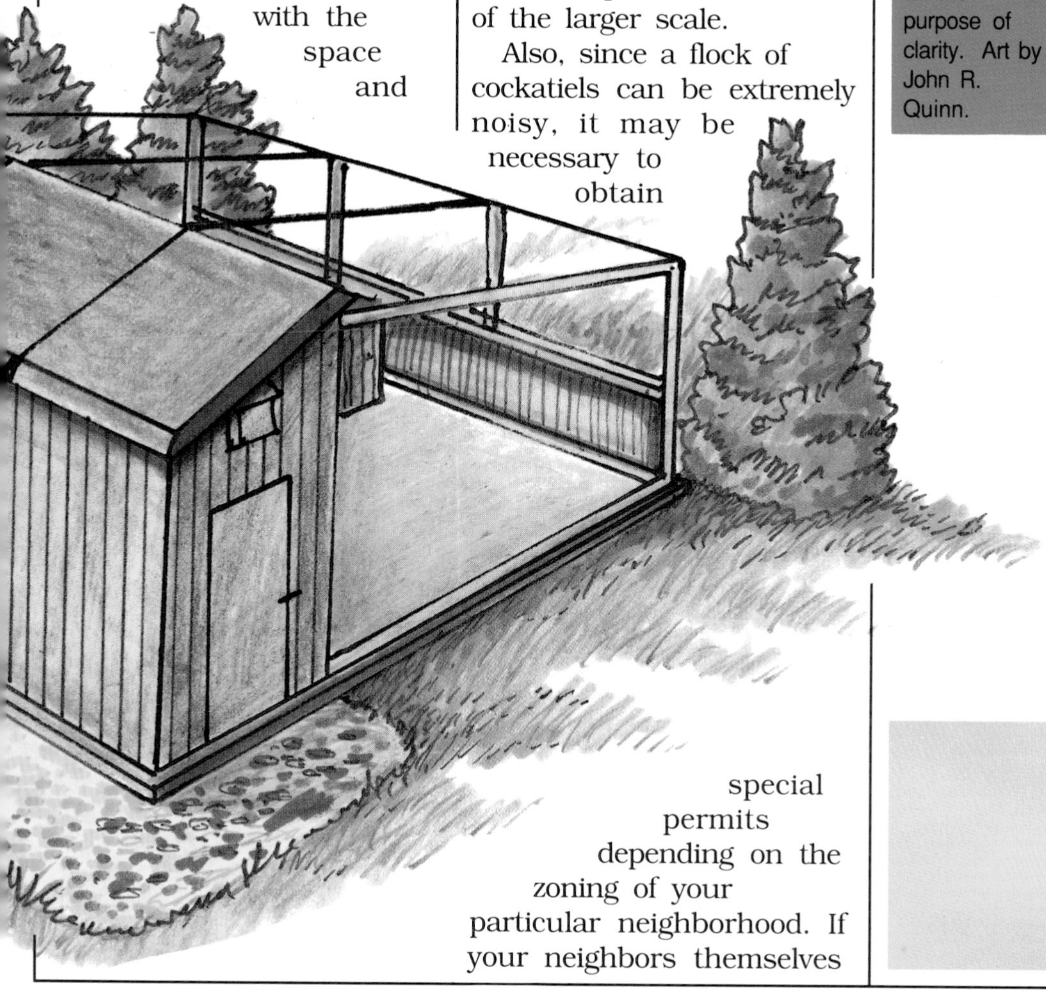

This suggested aviary design illustrates "the bigger the better" approach to cockatiel housing. The wire mesh has been omitted from the drawing for the purpose of clarity. Art by John R. Quinn.

are not bird lovers, you may also run into some problems if your animals begin to make a constant racket. Check out both of these concerns before you even break ground for an outside aviary.

The initial important requirement for an outdoor aviary is a suitable location. As is the case with smaller accommodations, you must find a site that is not exposed to too much direct sunlight or constant wind conditions. The midday shade of a large tree is often an ideal first consideration for such an outdoor aviary. The size of the aviary is, naturally, determined by the land space you have available. If you don't have a good 10 x 6 x 7-foot location, an outdoor aviary is probably not a good idea. The 10 x 6 x 7-foot size is adequate, but 30 x 10 x 12 feet would probably be even better. With these birds, the rule of thumb is often "The bigger, the better."

Garden supply stores, hardware stores, and similar establishments will be able to provide you with everything you will need if you plan on making the aviary yourself. The basic outdoor aviary should have an enclosed area for free-flying, called a "flight," and a shelter. The main framework for the full dimensions of the flight as well as the shelter itself can be constructed from hardwood timber, angle steel, or galvanized metal pipe. The flooring can be the natural soil or concrete covered with sand. Natural earth floors should be enclosed with brick or steel barriers above and below the ground to prevent snakes and rodents from entering. Many experts recommend the concrete floors, which are often sloped and constructed for easy drainage. These are excellent for sanitary conditions. Others feel that natural soil is better for the birds' general well-being.

If you go with a natural soil floor, some experts suggest raking the remains of the birds' food and some seeds into the earth. They will sprout in a relatively short time and

Facing Page, Above and Left: These photos show cockatiels maintained under ideal conditions: the roomy outdoor flight cage. The wild eucalyptus tree (left) has a cockatiel nesting cavity in its main crotch. Photos by Dr. Gerald R. Allen.

An affectionate pair of cockatiels cuddles up in an outdoor aviary. Photo by Dr. Gerald R. Allen.

will provide a vitamin-enriched dietary supplement. Since the cockatiel is primarily a ground feeding bird, many experts highly recommend the natural-earth flight floor. Also, the cockatiels will feel more secure in the flight if the perimeter is lined with low shrubbery.

If your choice is a concrete floor without any sand or soil covering, try to include a trough or large planter opposite the shelter for planting vegetable seeds. This, if filled with soil or sand and watered every day, will provide a green food supply for your birds. The minute particles of soil they will also eat will help them in grinding their food. Such a trough should be tended daily because the birds will chew up the plants in a very short period of time.

Perches in the aviary should be on the sides of the flight so they will not obstruct the already limited flying space. It is not a good idea to include any swinging perches. These have been known to injure inexperienced younger birds with unexpected movement. A continually renewed supply of fresh branches secured into the ground for the birds to chew on should be included. They enjoy stripping away the bark and chewing on the bare wood beneath. Eucalyptus trees are a special favorite since they are common in the birds' natural habitat.

The aviary shelter is basically for the birds' protection during bad weather. Depending on the kind of climate you live in, the shelter can be totally enclosed or partially opened. For cooler climates, a heating system might also be wise. Cockatiels can survive low temperatures as long as there are no drafts present, but in extreme conditions, a heating system might be a necessity.

The shelter roofs are often constructed of wallboard or galvanized iron with insulation. There should be a perch included in the shelter no more than a couple of feet from the ceiling. The shelter floor should also have a layer of gravel or sand spread out on it to help the birds' claws and feet.

An access walkway needs to be constructed around the aviary in such a way as to be able both to reach your birds and, at the same time, not allow any escape routes. Feeding is best done on feeding shelves located directly above low entrance doors. Since the birds themselves are the best judges of when they need some flying exercise, there should be an opening that will provide constant access for the cockatiels from the shelter to the flight and back again.

Another possible design for the outdoor aviary. Be sure to line the flight cage floor with an easily cleaned substrate. Art by John R. Quinn.

Feeding Your Cockatiel

Chow time for cockatiels! These birds have been offered a good variety of fare, including seeds , nuts, and a slice of apple. Food variety is the key to cockatiel health. Photo by Michael Gilroy.

Luckily for pet owners, cockatiels are easily satisfied when it comes to feeding, and their basic diet consists of ordinary seeds. As long as they are healthy, there should be no real problems in having them maintain a good diet. In the case of a single bird, the commercial variety of seed mixtures, consisting of sunflower seeds, red, yellow, and white millet, peanuts, hemp, oats, and wheat are perfect for their needs. These blends offer most of the birds' basic nutrients. Since, once opened, commercial feed can lose some of its nutritional value, you should buy only about one to two weeks' supply at a time. Be certain that the seed is stored in a dry place, in plastic or glass containers. Your local pet shop supplies exactly the kinds of containers you will need. This, with the addition of some fresh green food, should really be all that your bird will need.

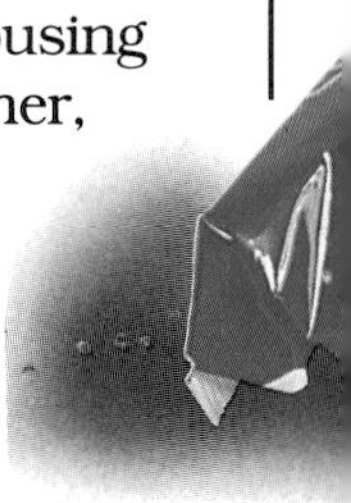

In the case of housing several birds together, it might be advisable to offer the different varieties in separate shallow and heavy dishes. This will assure that the birds enjoy different kinds of seeds in the necessary quantities and less is wasted by their natural tendency to scatter their food around. Different seeds are preferred by different birds, and their individual likes may fluctuate with the seasons and during breeding or molting seasons. The birds will scatter the unwanted varieties if they are included in the commercial feed. If ample room is provided on the birds' feeding shelf, the smaller types of seeds, such as millet, niger, canary seed, and linseed could be supplied there mixed. Sunflower seeds, should always be made available. Because of its high oil content, hemp must be used with caution. If given too much, the birds will gain unwanted weight. A certain amount of fat is healthy and necessary for the birds, so small portions of hemp should be made available just prior to breeding season or the cooler times of the year. Hulled and unhulled oats and other cereals such as wheat should be available at all times even if the birds initially refuse to eat them.

Millet sprays and honey sticks, available at pet shops,

Tortilla chips are not a recommended staple of cockatiel diet, no matter how much the birds may enjoy them. Photo by Michael Gilroy.

Cockatiels enjoy a treat of citrus, but as with other fruits included in the diet, don't overdo it. Photo by Michael Gilroy.

are also popular and acceptable sources of nourishment for your birds.

GREEN FOODS AND FRUIT

Supplementing the seeds, various green foods and certain varieties of fruit should also be provided. In season, the birds enjoy carrots, pears, and apples as well as berries such as rosehips, rowan, and hawthorn. Green food examples include watercress, thawed frozen peas, green corn, plantain, foxtail, thistles, chickweed, dandelion, carrot leaves, common groundsel, lettuce, and spinach. Unripened sunflower seeds are a special favorite. Since green food should be eaten by the birds only when it is fresh, make sure that all the uneaten portions are removed on a daily basis. When out of season, green food substitutes include sprouted seeds such as sunflower and oats. The required quantity of this kind of food should be soaked for 24 hours in water, rinsed well and left to stand for an additional 24 hours until it is just starting to sprout. Do not offer your cockatiel an overabundance of this treat.

When the birds are being reared, white bread and water-soaked wheat bread can be used as supplements to the diet. There is a wide variety of commercial rearing foods available. (Many of the commercial rearing foods must be moistened before they can be ingested by the birds.) You can also offer the birds the actual branches from freshly cut hazelnut, willow, or fruit trees.

CUTTLEBONE

The standard cuttlebone as well as available commercial calcium and mineral blocks will supply the birds with the needed calcium. Egg shells and grated mussel shells also are often used to supply this need.

Just as most animals do, cockatiels have an instinct that guides them as to the proper types and quantities of vitamins they need. There are, however, vitamin supplements available on the market. These should be offered only after consulting with your veterinarian. If they are to be used, you should do so only during the winter months. Overdosing is a danger with such vitamin preparations and possible premature molting may occur if these supplements are improperly given.

GRIT

Since birds have no teeth, they need something to grind up their food before it can be properly digested. Grit is used by cockatiels for this vital need. The grit is stored in the bird's gizzard after it is eaten. The action of the contraction and expansion of the muscular walls of the gizzard, combined with the coarse bits of grit, breaks up the food so it can enter the bird's stomach and be properly digested. It is, therefore, of vital importance that your cockatiel has a supply of grit and cuttlebone. Both of these supply needed minerals and trace elements. Most pet shops will carry the commercial grit and cuttlebone.

The grit should be in its own separate container on the floor of the cage or aviary and topped off occasionally. After about two months, the container should be cleaned and completely refilled.

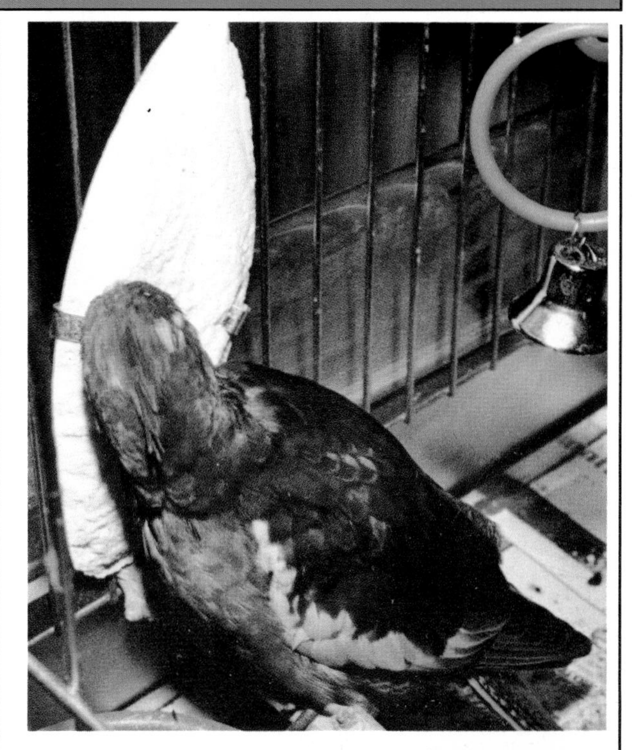

Cuttlebone is readily purchased at any pet shop and should be made available to your cockatiel at all times. Photo by Bruce D. Lavoy.

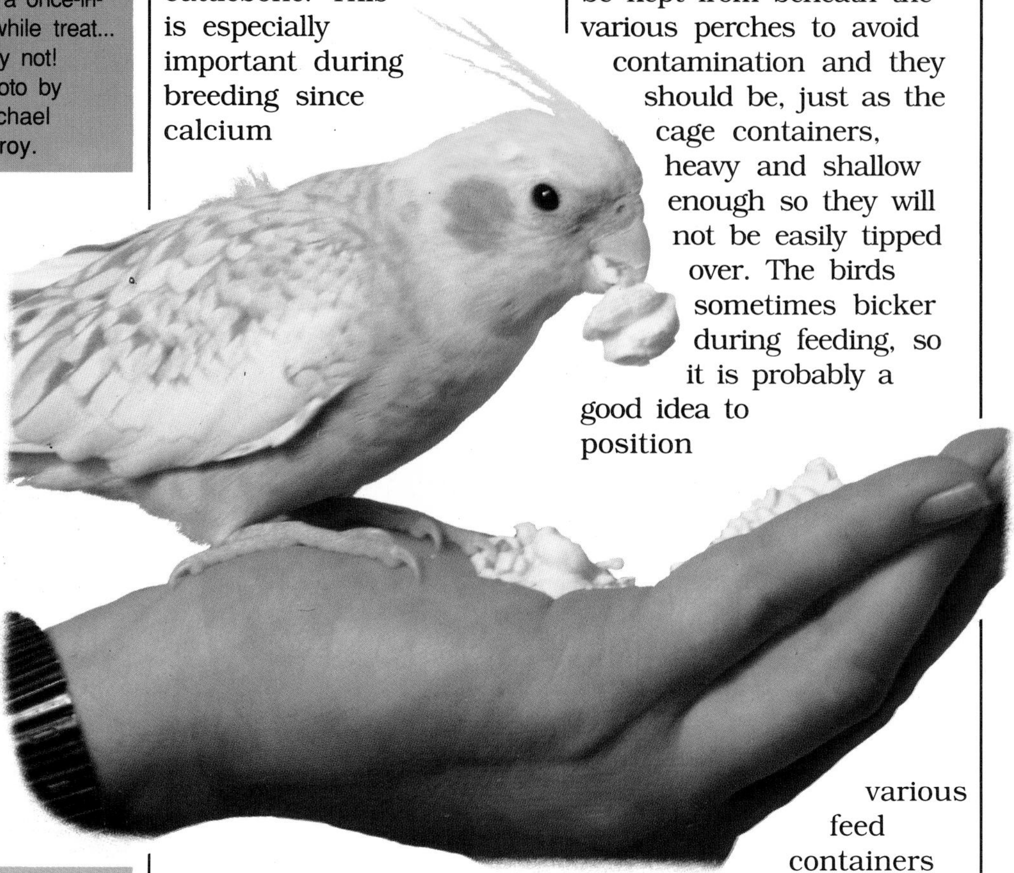

Popcorn is not very nutritious, but as a once-in-a-while treat... why not! Photo by Michael Gilroy.

Calcium is needed by cockatiels to maintain healthy beaks. The calcium requirements are met by the use of the standard cuttlebone. This is especially important during breeding since calcium is needed for the proper formation of the egg shells. Brooding birds will increase their use of the cuttlebone almost threefold over normal periods. Cuttlebones, with clips designed for attaching them to cages, are available at your local pet shop.

The feeding requirements for cockatiels in aviaries are the same as for a single pet bird in a cage. They should be fed once a day in either early morning or in the late afternoon. The containers of food should be kept from beneath the various perches to avoid contamination and they should be, just as the cage containers, heavy and shallow enough so they will not be easily tipped over. The birds sometimes bicker during feeding, so it is probably a good idea to position various feed containers at different spots around an aviary so that a number of birds can feed at once without getting in one another's way. Some breeders and cockatiel keepers have constructed special portable feed stations. These can be moved in and out of the shelter depending on the weather. They should be made with sliding trays for easy cleaning. Feeding stands should be supported by metal pipes so that mice and similar rodents, if they make their way into the aviary, cannot steal the food.

Fresh water should be available at all times, especially during warmer weather. Be sure to scour the container clean on a regular basis. Photo by Dr. Gerald R. Allen.

WATER

Cockatiels drink only water. Since their natural habitat in Australia is very dry, they have adapted in order to do without water for extended periods of time. They can sustain their needed water intake from a few drops of moisture on green food. Nevertheless, clean, fresh water should be constantly made available to them. Some people feel that a single container for both drinking and bathing is acceptable, although a pair of dishes is preferred by others. Even if you do supply two water dishes, the birds will probably use them both for drinking and bathing. Ideally, a fountain can be installed in an aviary.

While they can survive for considerable time without water intake, cockatiels' high metabolic rate burns up fat reserves rapidly. They would probably starve after only a single day without food.

It is always a good idea to find out exactly what diet your bird has enjoyed at its previous home. No matter if you've purchased your bird from a pet shop or a private owner, find out exactly what the bird has been eating. If it is a healthy bird, don't change the diet substantially unless it is completely necessary. If you do need to change the bird's diet, do so gradually, replacing the animal's old food with the new over a period of weeks.

Training Your Cockatiel

Second only to the budgerigar, the cockatiel is the most popular pet bird among people wishing to have a single bird. Not only is it a beautiful bird, but it also learns quickly, is reasonably priced, and is available in most good pet shops. It has a pleasant song to sing and can be taught to mimic the human voice and say a few simple words.

The first requirement before attempting to teach a bird to talk is to make certain it has been tamed. Luckily, the cockatiel is one of the easiest birds to tame. A young cockatiel must learn to trust its owner and be secure in its immediate environment. Birds 12 to 14 weeks old are usually the most responsive to training. Older birds are set in their ways or have been trained by a previous owner. They will resist retraining to a certain extent.

After your initial acquisition of your cockatiel, house the bird alone. Keep it separate from all other birds, both other cockatiels and birds of different species. You should have already decided on the bird's cage location and have it completely stocked with all necessities. Keep it there. Moving the cage from place to place after your bird has arrived will only upset the cockatiel.

You should exercise caution when transferring your new bird from its transport to its cage. Give the bird time to climb into the cage and become familiar with its new home, being certain there are no other birds or animals around. Avoid anything that would startle the bird and frighten it away from the cage. Leave it alone for awhile afterwards so it may

Opposite: A little interaction between pet owner and pet. **Above:** A pearl and a gray pied cockatiel share a perch. Photo by Isabelle Francais.

become comfortable in solitude. If it is night, keep a low light on in the room so the bird will be able to find its way around the new and unfamiliar surroundings.

Some experts feel that you should wait a week or more before trying to tame and teach your cockatiel. Many others believe that the birds need only a short time, sometimes only hours, before they will be ready for close human contact. However, during these first few days, always approach the bird quietly, talking softly until it appears calm. After a time, the bird will have learned that the cage is the place where it is fed and where it feels safe. Eventually, it will want to return to the cage on its own after an exercise flight. If you allow the cockatiel to go flying on its own before it has come to regard the cage as home, you will probably have to capture it and return it to the cage. This would cause the bird much agitation and only prolong the time it takes for it to become used to the cage, your home, and you.

In a very short while, the bird will begin to anticipate the approach of the owner, responding to the low talking with a soft whistling of its own. When this begins to happen, the first step in taming and training your bird has been accomplished.

Once used to its surroundings, the bird will be ready for taming. Quietly reach in and grasp the bird gently around the wings. It will most likely nip or bite you, but while these bites are sometimes painful, bites from younger birds rarely inflict any damage. If you maintain your gentle hold on the bird, it will soon realize that its pecking will do no good and it will stop. Older birds can bite with greater force and sometimes draw blood. If this happens, treat your injury as you

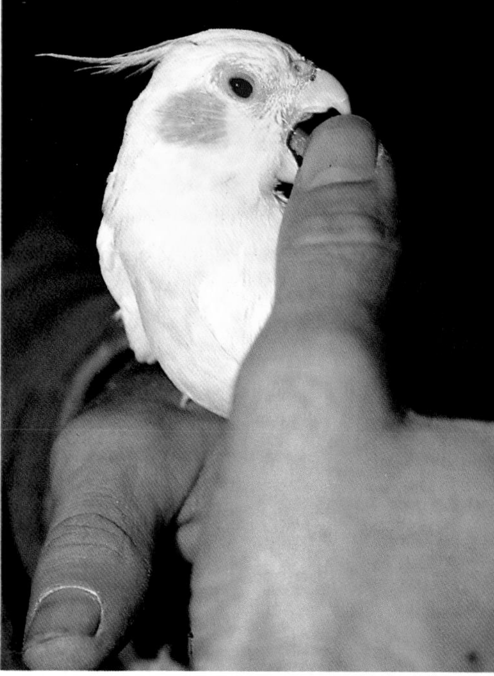

The bite of a young cockatiel will seldom break the skin, but an adult bird could inflict some damage. Photo by Van der Meid.

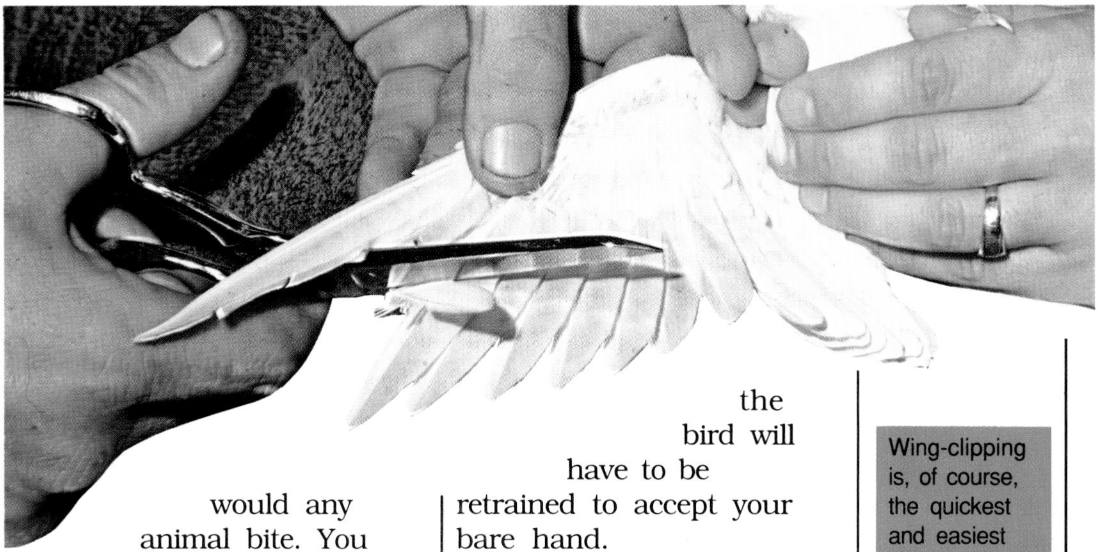

would any animal bite. You can force a cockatiel to release its beak by thumping it sharply beneath its chin. Avoid punishing the bird for its biting by hitting its beak or any other such practice. They are following inborn survival instincts. Punishment for these instinctive actions will cause the bird to develop a nasty personality and all training and taming efforts will become more and more difficult.

If you fear the bite of the bird, you can wear tight leather gloves, but keep in mind that the bird will have to be retrained to accept your bare hand.

WING CLIPPING

At this time, you may choose to clip the bird's wings. There are two schools of thought regarding this practice. Some hobbyists maintain that since cockatiels are much more oriented to flight than many omer parrots, wing clipping will deprive them of sufficient exercise. Others feel that wing clipping increases the ease of the taming process and prevents your bird from escaping. Wing

Wing-clipping is, of course, the quickest and easiest way to ground a cockatiel. The entire complement of primaries may be removed (below) or, in order to preserve the shape of the wing, only the middle primaries cut (above).

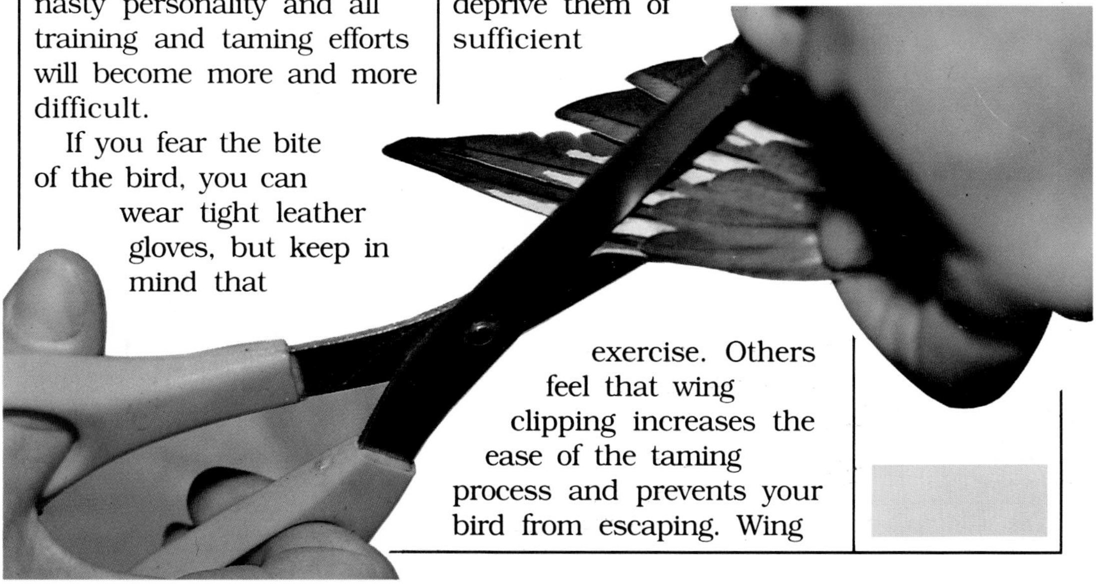

clipping is quick and painless, but easier if two people are involved: one to hold the bird securely while the other does the clipping. The one holding the bird gently extends the wings so all of the primary feathers can be cut from one side. This method will still allow the bird to fly with the other wing, although its flights will be greatly limited. Clipping does not detract from the cockatiel's beauty and the clipped feathers will grow back within six months. You can periodically clip the wings if you want to subdue its flying ability all the time, or you can simply let them grow back normally after the bird is fully trained. Whatever the case, the bird should never be allowed any amount of free flying time out of doors. No matter how well trained or tame it appears, outdoor flying will only end up with its becoming lost.

Other cockatiel keepers clip all of the primary feathers except the outer few, plus some of the secondary feathers. Done evenly, this will maintain the bird's graceful look while in flight and limit its flying ability at the same time.

Clip from the middle of the wing outward, level with the primary coverts. Don't cut too far under the coverts since the base of these feathers contains blood vessels. If bleeding does occur, watch it carefully, but do not be too concerned. Birds' blood coagulates rapidly and the bleeding should stop very shortly. It is very important that you make no

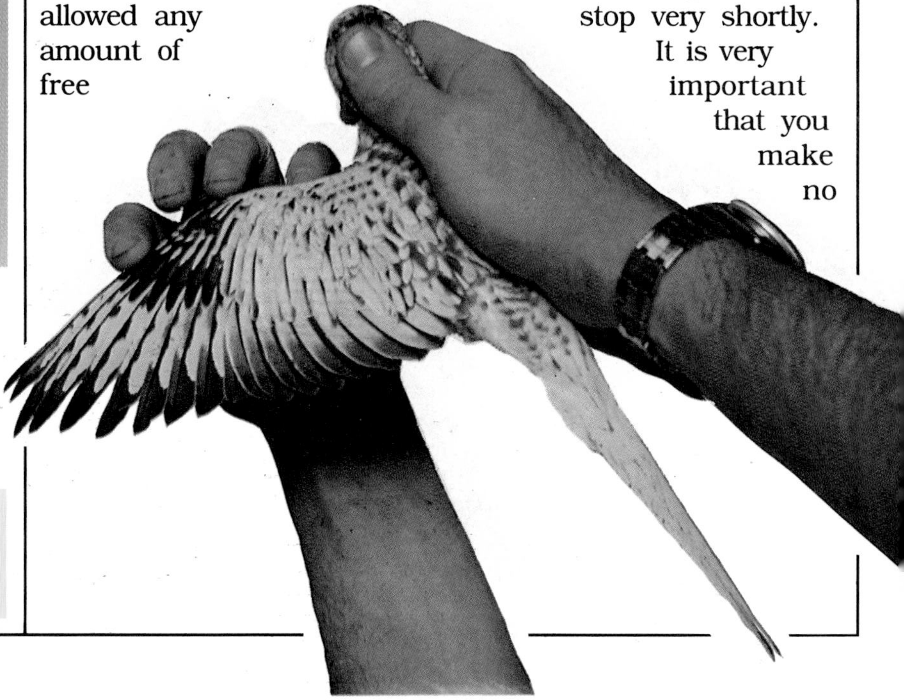

A bird's wing, fully spread and with feathering complete, is a thing of great natural beauty!

sudden movements during the clipping operation. Sudden movements or undue noise with the scissors will cause the bird to panic and serious injury may result.

If you're nervous about wing clipping, it might be wise to consult your pet shop owner or a bird expert either to do the clipping for you or to guide you through it.

The next step is to begin to offer the bird food from your hand. Hand feeding should begin through the bars, giving the bird millet sprays or other easily handled food. After a time, you can begin feeding it through the opened door. This should be done carefully and calmly. If you jump or make sudden movements, the bird will often panic. If it comes to associate these panicky moments with the feeding time, then you'll have lost all the ground you have gained in the training and taming process. If care and caution is

The moment of truth in hand taming: the cockatiel takes that first tentative step from the wood perch to the finger. Photo be Michael Gilroy.

A fully trained and tamed cockatiel will tolerate and even enjoy the most intimate handling by its owner. Photo by Michael Gilroy.

maintained, it won't be long before the cockatiel is eating out of your hand.

When this begins, you can further increase your bird's trust by gently stroking its breast with your index finger as it eats its treat. If the bird is not frightened by this action, you can increase the pressure until the bird is forced to step onto your finger as its perch to reach the food. At times, in the beginning, the bird might peck or bite your finger. This could be quite painful, but pulling away suddenly must be avoided. Again, sudden movements on your part will frighten and panic the bird, making it forget much of the trust you've worked hard to establish.

Constant repetition of the feeding and finger mounting routine will eventually have the bird hopping onto your finger immediately to get its treat. It will come to associate you and your hand with feeding time and be anxious to climb on. After a time, you can slowly move your hand from inside the cage, being continually careful not to make quick, jerky movements. Such actions will cause the bird to take to the air. Some birds enjoy being lightly scratched on the side and top of the head. This can further calm them as they eat from your hand. If you remove the bird slowly from the cage it will remain on your finger for a time. At times, a younger bird will jump from your hand and sit on the floor. If this happens, place your finger in front of it, down on its level, and coax it onto your finger once again. After a time, the bird will become used to the slow upward movement of your hand and remain perched. Since cockatiels constantly seek the highest point, they will begin to climb up your arm and sit on your shoulder. Later, they will try to reach the top of your head for the highest view. This will happen only if the bird has lost all of its fear of you. Old clothes are the order of the day in this case, since there are no records of any cockatiel having been successfully housebroken.

Never feed your bird outside of its cage. Your goal is to have your cockatiel associate feeding with the cage location so it will know that *that* is where it can find food. This will help convince the bird to return to its cage on its own after flights.

FREE FLIGHT TIME

Your bird must be allowed some free flight time at least once a day to maintain its well-being. It

Kids and cockatiels—a natural! A pet cockatiel is an ideal way to teach children the responsibility of caring for a small animal.

needs to exercise so it will not become overweight and it needs to satisfy its instinctive urge for free movement. The flight time *must* be supervised. The cockatiel is an inquisitive bird and will investigate just about anything with its strong and sharp beak. Unless you don't care about the furnishings in your bird's room, you will have to keep its flying time under close scrutiny.

Once out of its cage, the bird will start to fly. Before you even open the cage door, make certain that all doors and windows are closed. Also, be sure that clear window glass as well as wall mirrors are covered so that the bird will not mistake them for openings. They can collide with closed windows and be seriously hurt.

Remember that even though it may have become familiar with its cage at home, if it escapes to the outdoors, it will be completely disoriented by outside sights, smells, and sounds. It has no homing instincts and it is highly unlikely that it will ever find its way back home.

Unless the bird is hungry or thirsty, it will probably not return to its cage on its own after its first flight around its room. It will most likely find the highest

Opposite: Cockatiels are very swift and agile fliers, as is suggested in the tapered yet broad wings and the long slender tail feathers. **Below:** An empty coffee cup can't harm a curious cockatiel, but make sure that any objects or appliances that could are out of the way. Photo by Isabelle Francais.

Here's what it's all about–enjoying your appealing, affectionate pet cockatiel. This bird appears to be full-flighted. Photo by E. Goldfinger.

spot in the room and perch itself there to look over the surroundings. To lure it back, you might begin with the outstretched finger and, if it does step aboard, you could try, very slowly and cautiously, to move it back toward the cage-door opening. You should never try to chase or grab the bird. If you do, it will probably destroy the trust you have succeeded in building, and it will never return to your finger again.

If the finger method fails, wait until dark, shut off the light and grab the bird by throwing a cloth over him. He will not recognize this as your hand and his positive association will not be harmed.

Once the association of food and security is established between bird and cage, the cockatiel will return to its cage on its own when it's hungry or wants to rest.

As we noted before, cockatiels are sociable animals. They enjoy being with their own kind, of course, but if a bird

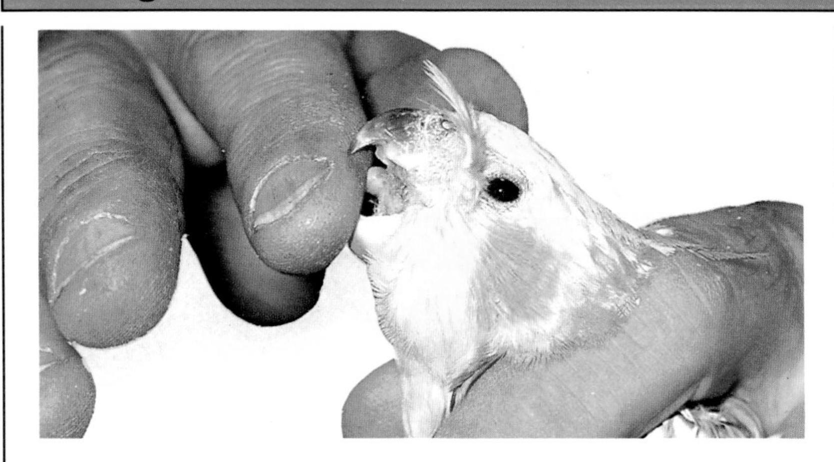

Biting the hand that feeds it? A young cockatiel cannot bite hard enough to draw blood, but a mature bird just might. Handle gently! Photo by Michael Gilroy.

is caged alone, it will soon transfer its affection to its human owner. This happens only if it receives enough attention. If the bird is ignored for any great length of time, it tends to become noisy and, at times, destructive. If you are attentive and loving to your pet, it will respond in kind.

Some of this affection might manifest itself in a strong desire to play with you. Cockatiels can be taught to mimic short tunes, speak a few words, and even perform a few simple tricks. The main requirement for teaching your bird any of these things is patience. Other requirements are that the bird be *very* tame and trust its owner completely. It is also very difficult to teach your bird anything if it is housed with another of its own kind. It will be more interested in the other bird than it will in you and any of your training efforts. The bird also has to have that certain *something*; that certain *ability* that allows it to learn and repeat the sounds it hears.

Repetition is the key word here. You have to repeat the words, phrases, or tunes many, many times in the bird's presence before it will begin to mimic what it hears. The birds are more receptive to this kind of training in the evening hours. The session should not really be longer than half an hour, but it can be done with the use of a tape recorder and a continual tape loop. Also, you should maintain a fairly regular schedule each night. This will cause the bird to anticipate the session and may speed up the learning process. Cockatiels, like most other birds and animals, have a very strong internal body clock.

At first, they might repeat the words or tunes in a

very indistinct manner, becoming clearer as they do it over and over again as they continue to hear the sounds. Do not try to start them out with complete and complex sentences or melodies. Some cockatiel owners have achieved success with the reward method, giving the bird a special treat whenever it finally repeats the desired song or words. Once it learns its first tune or phrase, others come easily. However, its memory has to be sparked continually, or it will forget the things it has learned. Cockatiels seem to prefer the higher-pitched voices of women and children.

The birds respond better if their immediate environment is kept clean, with uneaten seeds and molted feathers removed at least three times a week.

The teaching process can be a long one. Some birds will take months before they begin to imitate familiar sounds. Some never do. Again, patience will usually be rewarded, if not with actual recognizable sounds, then with affection because of all the attention you've been showing your pet cockatiel.

A mutual "cautious admiration" society? Cockatiels instinctively seek high places to perch; next stop, the owner's head! Photo by Dr. Herbert R. Axelrod.

Breeding Your Cockatiel

Cockatiels are considered one of the easiest pet birds to breed in captivity. Amateur aviculturists often turn to breeding their pets after only a short time of owning a single bird. If you are planning this exciting aspect of bird keeping, you will find it one of the most rewarding experiences you can have.

It is not our goal in this book to teach you to set yourself up as a pro fessional cockatiel breeder. The birds you see in your local pet store usually come from large aviaries, and the breeding techniques there vary somewhat from the information presented within these pages. We are directing our attention towards the pet owner rather than the professional aviculturist. There is nothing to prevent you from expanding on what you learn here by further reading or by consulting your pet shop owner or a professional bird breeder.

Once you have realized how fascinating and how much fun the cockatiel can be, you might be inspired to try breeding additional pets. It is

You must have been a beautiful baby? Nestling cockatiels leave a lot to be desired in the looks department, but few people are disappointed in the end result! Photo courtesy Vogelpark Walsrode.

Cockatiels in the act of mating. Photo by Dr. Gerald R. Allen.

essential that you start out with a pair of happy, contented, trustful birds. This is the first and one of the most important steps in a successful breeding attempt. In some countries it is necessary to obtain a license to breed birds. Check with your local pet shop owner regarding any requirements you may have to meet before beginning.

As mentioned previously, sexing your bird and its potential mate may be difficult. A common wild-colored cockatiel is the easiest since the males have the yellow head and the females have more gray. The other color varieties may prove more difficult to identify. Methods for identifying sex include pulling a flight feather off and seeing what color the new one that grows back will be, or feeling the pelvic bones (females have light-colored stripes or spots on their feathers and their pelvic bones are wider and more flexible than their male counterparts). However, these methods are not infallible unless practiced by an expert. It's best to consult a professional breeder or your local pet shop proprietor.

It's best to make sure the birds you've paired for breeding are at least one year of age or older. Making certain you have mature cockatiels will also help to avoid such problems as unfertilized clutches and incomplete incubations. Younger birds are able to breed, but they have not proven to be the best parents.

If you have maintained the proper diet for your birds, and if their climate is carefully controlled, then they can breed at almost any time of year. It has been noted, however, that the first attempt at breeding is usually more successful if it takes place in the spring or in the early summer months. You must also be certain that you have a generous supply of fresh green food, grit mixture, cuttlebone, and seed grasses for a successful nesting period. These warming months are the best times of the year for obtaining fresh supplies of these important items. Birds raised indoors have not adapted their habits to the change of seasons. This is why pet cockatiels can usually be bred all year 'round.

Cockatiels can have more than one brood per year, but anything over two is dangerous. This tends to tire out the parents. Since the entire breeding cycle, from the courting of the parents to the weaning of the chicks takes about two and a half months, it is the normal practice to wait another two and a half months before allowing them to breed again. Since they will not breed unless they have a suitable nesting area, all you need do to prevent breeding is to remove the nest box.

Breeding indoors during the winter will present less danger of egg binding and less chance of the birds' developing mites. Mites in

Left: A pipped cockatiel egg on the verge of hatching. Photo by Bruce D. Lavoy. **Below:** This rather disheveled-looking chick is about 20 days old.

the summer will make the birds scratch themselves, and perhaps their eggs as well. You must be certain that your birds do not have any sign of mites before the breeding process is even begun. If you happen to find that your birds are suffering from mites during the

incubation period, you should spray them with a mite spray (available at your pet store). This should be done outside the nest box so that you will not damage any of the eggs. To further prevent the onslaught of mites, spray the nest box and the entire cage before setting them up together. The nesting activities of the parents are increased to such a degree that it is very difficult to keep their immediate environment clean during this period. It's best to start out as clean and as sanitary as possible for the safety of the parents as well as the newly hatched chicks.

Keep the bottom of the cage clean during incubation and remove perches for daily cleaning as well. Don't attempt to give the entire cage a thorough cleaning during this time since all that activity will upset and agitate the parents.

Mites are not the only difficulty encountered during summer breeding. The heat might also cause the cockatiels to abandon the nest and the eggs. Trial and error might be the only way to determine the best breeding time for your particular cockatiel pair.

DIET SUPPLEMENT FOR BREEDING BIRDS

To further aid the birds in becoming prepared for breeding, a supplementary addition to their diet, consisting of mineral-enriched foods is recommended. A week's supply of this supplement includes one-quarter cup of parakeet seed, one-third cup oats, one-half cup commercial nesting food, and one-quarter cup of conditioning food. All of these are available at your local pet store. These ingredients should be mixed

Opposite: The cockatiel nest box should be roomy, affording both birds enough room to move about without damaging the eggs. Photo by Michael Gilroy. **Left & Below:** Variety is the spice of life—and of the balanced cockatiel diet. The conventional seed and nut mix can be varied with any number of garden vegetables.

together in a separate container and placed in the food dish with about four drops of wheat germ oil sprinkled over it just prior to the birds' feeding.

The rest of their diet should remain the same as during normal periods, but kept in a separate dish. Lettuce and carrots should be included in the breeding pair's diet to keep their bowels loose. If they develop constipation, add a few drops of lime to their drinking water supply.

Breeding cockatiels need a certain amount of freedom beyond the normal daily flying exercises. They should never be confined to their cage for long periods of time. They must feel as free during this time as they would in their own natural habitat. If available, it is a good suggestion to have them set up in a room all their own, with their cage door left open. Any spare room that is not frequented by constant comings and goings of people will probably do. Their increased activity and chewing urges during these times increase their naturally untidy habits. You must realize this before you sacrifice the furniture in any given room to a pair of breeding cockatiels. Extra caution must be taken in these cases to make sure the birds do not escape when anyone is entering or leaving the room.

The extra exercise is recommended to offset the richness of the necessary breeding diet. It is potentially dangerous for your birds if they gain too much weight during the nesting period.

Below: That cockatiels are active, inquisitive, and diligent chewers can be readily observed in this bank of well-worn nest boxes. **Opposite:** Nest boxes may take any shape and form desired–from standard construction to the hollowed-out log type. The small objects in the foreground are finch nesting cups, not suitable for cockatiels. Photos by M. Vriends.

NEST BOXES

Unless a suitable nesting area is provided, the birds will not breed at all. You can buy a wooden nest box for your breeding pair at your pet shop. This should be placed near or on top of the cage, in a location the birds can easily see during flight and easily accessible at all times. Try and place it near a wall away from drafts and so that the birds will be aware in advance of anyone approaching. The hen is very cautious and wary during the breeding periods, so the nest box has to be an inviting and safe place for her to nest.

If you are constructing the nest box yourself you can use wood or chipboard, but avoid using newer materials which may have been chemically treated in some manner or have fresh glue on them. The birds' chewing on treated wood may cause harm. The box should be at least 16 inches in all directions. Be certain that all the joints are secure and tight since loose joints may allow drafts to enter, which could be disastrous to new chicks. The nest box must be able to retain the heat given off by the parents to properly incubate the young. There should be no gaps where chicks could catch their tiny claws. Wood screws are preferred over nails since they better secure the joints and are easier to remove if the box has to be disassembled for any reason.

A 3.5-inch hole should be at the center of the front of the box with a perch on the outside enabling the cockatiels to enter easily. This perch should also extend into the box for a few inches so the parents will not injure

These chicks, already well-sprouted in pin feathers, are being hand-reared in this basket. Photo by Michael Gilroy.

young chicks when they land inside. If the entrance is too narrow, both birds may try to enter or leave simultaneously, damaging the eggs in the process. Damaged eggs can be repaired with clear fingernail polish if they are discovered in time before too much vital fluid has been lost. In most cases, discovery of damaged eggs comes too late. The best preventative is to make certain your nest box is large and roomy enough.

A partition should be placed in the center of the nest box so that the forthcoming eggs will not roll around too much. Since both the cock and the hen incubate the eggs, the nest box has to be large enough for both birds to have room to move about unobstructedly.

You should also have an access door in the box so you can reach inside to monitor the new chicks. This is normally done by hinging the top so it can be slowly lifted and securely closed.

The well-constructed nest box is a proven winner when it comes to breeding cockatiels at home. It is almost impossible to reconstruct the nesting areas of the wild Australian cockatiels, so there is little reason to attempt it. Also, there is a danger that natural logs may be infested with mites. The birds will easily accept the box if it meets the afore-mentioned basic requirements. The nest box provides hours of privacy for the parents-to-be and

This brood clearly illustrates the fact that cockatiel eggs hatch progressively, as the eggs had been laid. The largest chick is about five days old, while the tiny youngster next to it is only minutes out of the egg.

will also serve as the first home for the chicks until they are old enough to leave and be on their own.

All of this increased freedom, the change in diet, and the presence of a nest box will, in turn, increase the birds' copulation period. Once all of this has been established, some breeders feel it is wise to examine the vent areas of your birds to make certain they are not obstructed by an overgrowth of feathers. Others say that it is best to leave well enough alone and let nature take its normal course. If you feel there is a problem in such a case, consult your pet shop owner.

Once the nest box is placed in position, the birds will begin a thorough investigation, the male usually doing the initial inspection. They both will scratch and chew on it and move all about it to see exactly what this new addition is. Eventually, the male will coax the female to join him inside. Since the normal gathering of nesting material is impossible for pet cockatiels, you will have to provide these much needed materials. Peat fibers that have been slightly dampened, wood shavings, sawdust, bark, dry leaves, or other soft material should cover the floor of the nest box at about an inch depth. Don't bother arranging this material in any particular fashion, as the birds will instinctively manage this task on their own. Avoid the use of cloth or cotton

A newly-hatched brood of cockatiels. The parents and young should be disturbed as little as possible; check the youngsters only when the parents are out of the box. Photo be Dr. Gerald R. Allen.

for nesting material.

When courting begins, you will see your pair of cockatiels preening, kissing, snuggling, and feeding each other. They are not nervous about courting in front of humans. It will be obvious to you that they enjoy each other's company. You might see them having slight disagreements, but they will soon continue their happy pair-bonding rituals.

Copulation will continue right up until the hen lays her first egg. A few days prior to this, she will lose much of her interest in the advances of the male. The times between copulation will increase. The more obvious signs of an imminent egg include the female's labored breathing and her bloated-looking body. She will sit hunched on her perch and ruffle her feathers frequently. Her tail feathers might appear a bit ragged, but this is due to the increased activity of preparing the nesting material rather than as a direct result of her condition.

The hen will come out of the nest box a couple of times a day for her bath. Keep her water at room temperature so she can use it to keep her eggs moist and to prevent egg binding.

On the day the eggs are laid the parents will generally remain in the nest box except for occasional feeding

The eggs of cockatiels, like those of other cavity nesters, such as owls, have no need of protective coloration and thus are plain white. Photos by Dr. Gerald R. Allen.

This parent bird is clearly unhappy about being disturbed.

excursions. The hen is especially interested in calcium and grit during the entire incubation period.

Generally there are four or five eggs in a cockatiel clutch, but those in captivity, with more balanced diets and routines than their relatives in the wild, have been known to lay as many as eight. The hen will position herself in the corner of the nest box, place her head near the floor and prop her tail on the side of the box. It sometimes takes an hour to lay a single egg. She will do this approximately every other day until the clutch is complete. When each egg is laid, the hen will move it to the center of the box, and then tuck it under her breast. When it is time for her to lay another egg, the cock takes over warming the previous ones. At times, the hen may initially ignore the first few eggs. Do not be concerned if this occurs. She and the cock will begin the incubation when more eggs are laid.

If egg-binding does occur, and the hen becomes egg bound, gently hold her over warm steam. This will loosen the egg so she can comfortably lay it. If this is left unattended, the hen will be dead within a day. There is no oral medication that can prevent egg-binding.

Most experts agree that the eggs should be left in the care of the parents until they are hatched. Removing the eggs and substituting plastic replicas and replacing them when it is time for the full clutch to hatch, as has been the practice in some aviaries, results in all the chicks being hatched at the same time. This might tire out the parents and they may abandon one or more of the newborn chicks in order to keep up with the demands of the majority. The hen also may be able to sense that her eggs have been moved and will sometimes leave the chicks before they are able to fend for themselves.

The parent birds share the duties when it comes to keeping the nest of eggs warm. During the day, the female enjoys her renewed freedom, flying, eating, bathing, and generally going through the normal routine she employed before the breeding period began. The cock will spend the days sitting on the eggs. At times, the female will replace him for a short while during the day so he can eat, but the majority of the day is the male's time with the eggs.

When night falls, the hen resumes her incubation duties while the male stands guard. He will position himself outside the box near the entrance. The females, especially those incubating their first or second brood, are extremely reluctant to leave their nests. Sometimes the pair will divide up the eggs and share the incubation simultaneously.

During this time it is important that the parents be fed properly. Improper feeding may lead to the parents not feeding their young after the chicks hatch. The chicks are fed by the hen regurgitating her own food. If she hasn't been receiving the food she needs, she is not going to pass the proper nourishment on to her young.

After about a week has passed, you can check the eggs for fertility by holding an egg up before a pen light. If it appears to be about half full, then the egg is fertile.

Also, if the

There's scant beauty to be seen in very young cockatiels, but by the time they reached the age of twenty days, they have acquired the appeal of their parents. Photos by Dr. Gerald R. Allen.

egg has developed for four or five days, dark blood vessel branchings are also visible. To be certain all the eggs you're examining are at least the required week old, don't bother checking any of them until seven days after the last egg has been laid. The eggs are very fragile and must be handled with extreme caution. Improper handling, improper diet, and incomplete copulation are some of the known causes for infertile eggs.

About a week before the first eggs are due to hatch, place in the cage a dish containing an equal mix of baby cereal, strained bananas, and nesting food. Wet down this mixture slightly with water and add a couple of drops of wheat germ oil. This will supplement the birds' diet and help prevent their not feeding the coming chicks.

Anywhere from 18 to 21 days after the first egg is laid, you will begin to hear the chicks chirping from inside the shell and see a tiny hole appear in the eggshell. In a few hours, the chick will have completely hatched, and the hen will begin cleaning and feeding her new offspring. The hen will remove the membrane material from the chick and will feed it by regurgitating her own food. In order to transfer the food from the parent's beak to the chick's, the parent will grasp the chick's beak firmly and shake its head up and down vigorously. The food will drop from the parent's crop into the chick's. Always leave the parents

Hand feeding young cockatiels.

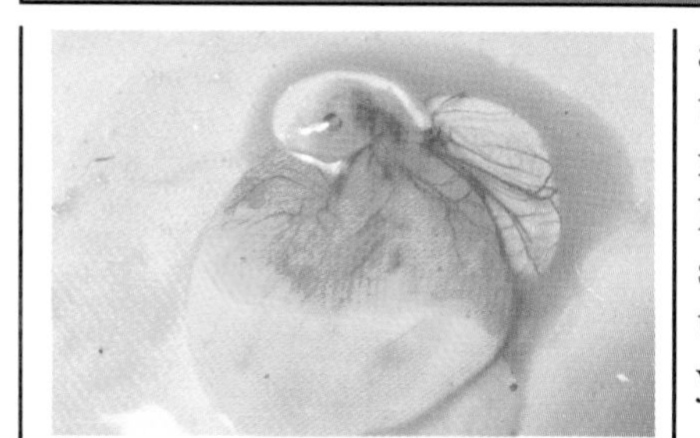

Cockatiel embryo

Four days old.

and new chicks alone during this important time.

Since the birds are feeding for their chicks as well as themselves, it is more important than ever to make certain the cage is well supplied with food. The young birds will ask to be fed by giving off a loud shriek. They will continue to beg their parents for food even after they have begun to eat on their own.

When they hatch, the young cockatiels are almost completely covered with down, pale yellow in color. They have a small bald patch on the back of their heads. The recognizable cheek patches will appear after about three weeks, and the full plumage will have developed in the fourth week. Their beaks are pink at first, turning brown and then dark after about three months. They will utter a loud croaking or hissing sound when you inspect them and may even peck at your hand initially.

On occasion, if the hen has not had the recommended bath times, the eggshells might be too hard and a hatching chick will become stuck. The parents will throw these eggs from the nest. It is very important to remove these eggs from the nesting area since a parent who has been picking at an egg may attack healthy ones.

Some bird keepers have tried to artificially incubate these damaged eggs by rubbing them with a wet cloth and heating them under a light bulb, but have had little success.

Nine days old.

Twelve days old.

Young cockatiels put on size quickly, as may be seen from this series of photos. By the age of 10 days, most of the down has disappeared, having been replaced by contour feathers.

By the age of twenty-two days, the young cockatiel is at least a fair approximation of its parent.

Fifteen days old.

Nineteen days old.

Do not become alarmed at the droppings of the parents during the incubation period. Instincts drive the parent cockatiels to keep the nest box extremely clean during this time. They will hold their droppings and expel them far away from the nesting area. This causes the droppings to be large, loose, and lighter in color than at normal times. The increased intake of calcium will also show up in the droppings as a whitish material.

Even extremely friendly and tame birds will become over-excited during the incubation time. They are instinctively protective of their young. During this time it is doubly important to remember that you should never come upon the birds suddenly. They should be made aware of your approach. Since they spend a great deal of time inside the nest box, caring for their young, it is suggested that you sing softly or whistle as you come closer so that they will realize someone is coming. If you use the familiar songs or words that you have taught them during training, they will come out to greet you or to receive their treat, whatever your routine has been prior to breeding. Once they are out, this will give you an excellent opportunity to inspect the new chicks.

There have been many instances where young chicks have been injured or killed by falling on or smothering in broken shell

Twenty days old.

Twenty-two days old.

fragments. The parents will try to push the fragments away from their young, but they are not 100% successful all of the time. Always be certain to remove shell fragments when the parents are outside the box.

It is also important to remove any food the hen has spilled on the chicks while feeding them. This regurgitated food is sticky and the parents have been known to accidentally harm or kill chicks trying to remove it after feeding. Clean the chicks off with a small ball of cotton soaked in warm water. Clean the beak and claws as well, dry the chick thoroughly, and return it to the nest box as soon as possible to prevent any drafts chilling the hatchling. It doesn't take a drastic chill to kill a newborn cockatiel.

After a little more than a week's time, you will see the chicks begin to develop their contour feathers, which at first look like prickly quills. They'll first show up on the crest, shoulder, and on the upper section of the tiny wings. When these quills develop further and unfold, the plumage will be revealed. The tail, throat, and cheek feathers will appear next, with the ones on the back showing up last.

The chicks' cries will be heard after only a few days and then only as a guttural purring sound and a series of peeps while being fed.

Parent cockatiels may continue to feed their offspring after they have fledged. Photo by Dr. Gerald R. Allen.

After about five or six weeks, the chicks will begin to leave the nest box, usually coaxed to the entrance by their father, and will begin eating seed and grit from the cage floor. They will learn this by observing their parents. Once they are eating on their own, they can be placed in their own cage.

It's best to make certain this first brood of chicks are separated from their parents before a second brood is expected to hatch. When they are first on their own, these young cockatiels will be extremely wild and their flying will appear very clumsy. They learn to fly more gracefully in a very short time. Some young birds are excellent flyers from their first flight.

Eventually, the young birds will learn to eat from their food dishes. In the meantime, sprinkle their seed and grit on the floor of their new homes. Since the birds will drop seeds into their water dishes, they should be changed several times a day. The water dishes should be small so the birds are not able to walk through them. Wet feet will make them susceptible to colds, which could prove fatal.

Young chicks are not that sure-footed. They will fall off higher perches unless they slowly learn how to retain their balance on one that is placed on

This trio of young birds is nearly fully feathered except for their rather short crests. Photo by Michael Gilroy.

the floor of the cage first. They will fall off these floor perches at first, but a daily half hour's training should teach them to stand on the dowel or fresh branch. In a couple of days, they should be standing on the perch on their own. You can help the birds gain confidence at higher and higher levels by supplying a small ladder like those available in your local pet store. The cockatiel will instinctively seek the highest level and will soon be able to stand on elevated perches. When the birds totally ignore the floor perch, you can remove it and raise their food dishes to higher levels as well.

HAND-REARING

There have been instances where the parents of newborn chicks have abandoned them. This has been known to occur in the case of younger parents. Whatever the cause, if it happens, you will be forced to hand-rear

"How'm I doin'?" This young cockatiel owner seems pleased that he's managed to keep his pet in place on the hand for so long! Photo by Michael Gilroy.

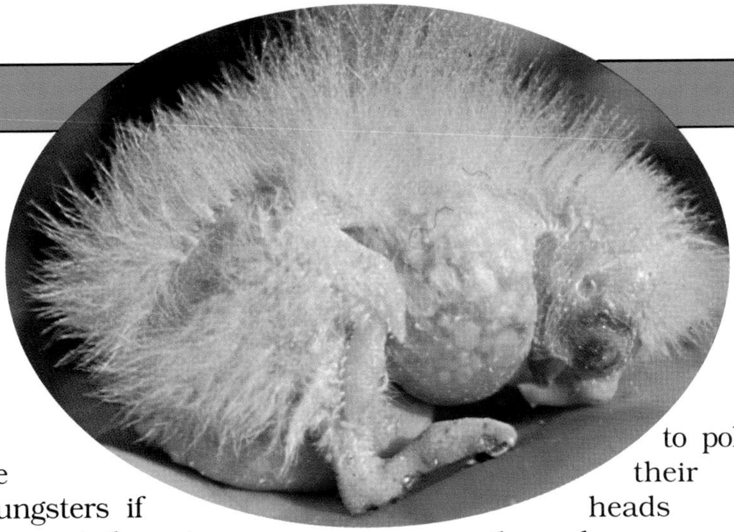

The ingested food can be clearly seen through this chick's distended crop. Photo by Dr. Herbert R. Axelrod.

the youngsters if you want them to survive. A cardboard or wooden box about 12 inches square with a layer of sawdust, dry leaves or sand on the bottom is an ideal new home for these abandoned chicks. Some breeders suggest using just a folded paper towel to line the bottom of the brooder box since this is easier to deal with when cleaning. Keep this brooder box covered and warm since any sort of chill is dangerous to the newborns. Hanging a small thermometer on the side of the box will help you to be sure that a temperature of 85° F. is maintained. Make sure that the thermometer is secure and out of reach of the chicks. If it falls to the bottom of the box they will certainly soil it and may be injured by it during their exploration of their home. Be certain that there are small breathing holes in the sides and the top of the box. These shouldn't be large enough for the chicks to poke their heads through.

Some bird keepers who have to hand-rear young cockatiels have suggested setting the box on a small electric heating pad. This should be done only if the box is separated from the pad by a towel and the pad is kept on a very low setting. If the temperature is too high for the chicks, they will begin to pant with their mouths open.

Naturally, you will have to hand-feed these youngsters. There are different methods of accomplishing this, some more successful than others. Some have had success with an eye dropper, but the most widely used method is with the help of a syringe with rubber tubing over the tip to prevent injury to the bird.

Prepare a formula from a mixture of lukewarm water, various green food, grated carrots, baby food, etc. One specific recipe calls for one-half cup high-protein baby cereal, one-half pint yogurt, one-half cup wheat germ, one-half cup bread crumbs, two drops of vitamins, a hard-boiled egg and a cup of lukewarm water. After four days you can add a half teaspoon of brewer's yeast and a half teaspoon of wheat germ oil to this mixture. After a week, half a jar of strained baby food carrots, a tablespoon of honey and two tablespoons of smooth peanut butter can be included. These ingredients should be pureed in a blender until they become thick and liquid. This will probably stay fresh for about three days refrigerated. After that time, make a fresh supply and discard the old mixture.

Using the syringe, this mixture should be fed to the chicks, drop by drop, into their beaks, every two to three hours during the day. You shouldn't have to feed them during the night as they will naturally be sleeping. After about four weeks you can cut back and feed them every four to six hours. You will have to hold their heads between your thumb and index finger. Their heads normally bob up and down during feeding, so you have to have them gently secured. Don't force their mouths open.

This lutino cockatiel is enjoying a treat of commercial bird kibble. Photo by Michael Gilroy.

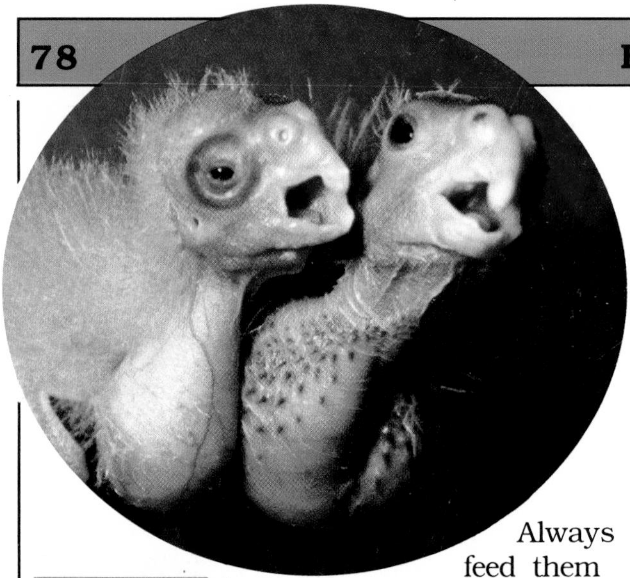

"Where's dinner?" These youngsters are about three days old.

Always feed them on a soft surface such as a rolled up towel. If they are set down on a slippery surface, their newborn legs will not be able to support their weight and they will slide all over the place.

The chick will normally make a chirping sound while you're feeding it and an air bubble may be formed in the crop. This is easily visible through the chick's almost transparent skin, so working the bubble up with your thumb and index finger should not be difficult. This will cause the chick to burp and allow it to continue to eat until its crop is full.

Make sure the feed mixture is warm since baby cockatiels won't eat cold food and it may also sour their crop, causing difficulties and possibly death if not treated. When finished, wash the chick off with a cotton swab and warm water, making certain that the inside of the beak is clear of food as well. Feed one chick at a time so the others will remain warm.

If you are feeding more than one chick, keep an extra syringe in a glass of warm water. When they grow a bit bigger, and you have added more food to the birds' diet, you can switch to using a spoon for feeding. You'll have better results with a plastic spoon clipped as close as you can into the shape of an adult cockatiel's beak. This will make it easier for both you and the young chick.

This young cockatiel being fed by its parent is fully fledged and of adult size! Photo by Dr. Gerald R. Allen.

After you've fed all the chicks, clean out their brooder box as best you can. Their droppings will be loose and soft and they will become very difficult to clean at mealtime if they are permitted to move around in a soiled box. As they get older, you should clean the box more often, not only at feeding times.

After about four or five weeks, when the birds are feathered out, you should wean them. Begin by cracking one-fourth cup of budgerigar mix with a rolling pin and sprinkling it on the floor of the cage with a bit of grit mixed in. Mixing the food ingredients by hand (instead of using the blender) makes a mash rather than a puree. Eventually, the birds will begin cracking the seeds on the bottom of the cage to eat the kernel. First they will consider the seed playthings and carry them around in their mouths. When you see that they have learned to eat this food, they are weaned, even if they still cry to be hand-fed. You can begin to play with the chick during the former feeding time and it will come to associate play with these periods rather than eating. In a few days, it will be on its own.

With the extended time you'll be spending with the birds, you'll actually watch them grow and will be amazed at how fast they turn into full grown and beautiful cockatiels. This is a hard and time-consuming task, but hand-reared birds reward you by forming a very close relationship with their keeper. They are extremely tame and make excellent cage birds. They have, after all, been completely dependent on you in order to live.

Just as in preparing foods for human consumption, cleanliness is the watchword in handling foods destined for cockatiels. Photo by Fred Harris.

A fine example of the wild-type cockatiel color variety. Photo by Michael Gilroy.

Breeding for Color

While breeding for color is a genetic science of major interest to professional cockatiel breeders, we feel we must mention it here since the chicks your birds will hatch depend on the variety with which you begin. To predict what color varieties will appear in any given brood requires a knowledge of the laws of genetics and accurate breeding records showing the ancestry of each parent bird in question. If you desire such controlled breedings, it's best to consult an expert cockatiel breeder or begin with questioning your local pet shop owner.

The most commonly colored cockatiel is the wild-colored bird, which is gray with the yellow crests and flame-orange cheek patches. Breeders use these birds to improve the size and type of the birds in the different color lines.

The albino cockatiel with red eyes was the first noted mutation, appearing around 1959. Not a pure white, the birds still maintain the recognizable cheek patches, the yellow crest, and light yellow tail feathers. Some of these birds have featherless patches on their heads behind the crest. Breeders avoid using these unfeathered birds for fear the baldness may be inherited by offspring, regardless of their color. There are also white cockatiels with black eyes, but these are not true albinos, having a completely different genetic history.

An albino cockatiel chick, showing the featherless spot on the head prevelant in this variety. Photo by Michael Gilroy.

Lutino cockatiels are yellow albinos with red eyes. They appear to be albinos with more yellow coloring on all of their feathers.

The cinnamon or isabella cockatiels are silver colored and considered very attractive. The head, forehead, cheeks, and chin are yellow with the crest being brown with yellow tips. The cheek patches are the standard flame-orange. The areas that are gray in the wild-colored birds are more brown in this variety. Their wings are cinnamon with light yellow patches. These variations make the bird appear cinnamon colored all over at a distance. Lighter varieties appear to be more cream colored than cinnamon.

Pearled cockatiels have plumage of a slightly lighter shade than the wild colored birds and have white and yellow spots on the upper sides of their wings. Their crests are gray with the standard yellowing showing only at the roots of the crest feathers. They have been noted with both black and red eyes, black being more common.

Bordered cockatiels are similar to the pearled variety, but the back and wing feathers have a dark or light margin to them. These colors tend to fade with age, however.

Pied cockatiels appear in various colors covering

A gorgeous duo of cinnamon lutinos. Photo by Michael Gilroy.

about 50% of their bodies. Most of the more striking birds have the yellow crests, but some have only yellow flecks. The white pied birds have a few gray feathers.

With controlled genetic breeding continuing, there may be other varieties that will show up in the years to come. Genetics is not an exact science, and experts feel that there are more surprises coming up from the differently bred cockatiels.

Keeping Your Cockatiel Healthy

Cockatiel owners are lucky, since their birds are very hardy and highly resistant to disease. Because of their long history in the wild, they have developed resistance to many of the common ailments that other caged birds fall victim to much more readily. It is not uncommon for cockatiels to live out their entire life spans without ever being sick. Despite this, they are known for being able to come down with a common cold or intestinal disorders.

Hopefully, you should have come home with a healthy bird. However, there is always the chance that disease may attack it at some later date. If you already have a cockatiel (or if you're planning to house your new bird with others),

The gray pied cockatiel, one of the more popular strains in the hobby. Photo by Michael Gilroy.

No, this preening cockatiel is not chained to its perch—the heavy chain holds the perch together! Photo by Michael Gilroy.

it is a wise suggestion to keep the new bird(s) separated from the ones already in your cage or aviary. This way, you can see if any problems arise before they have a chance of spreading to your healthy stock.

You can easily tell if your cockatiel is sick since they are all known to react in similar fashion. They will be stationary and fluff their feathers out, hiding their heads in their plumage in their attempt to retain as much body heat as they can. They will often display a runny nose or reddened eyes. Their general movement will be apathetic and you can see them shiver visibly. Loose droppings can be an indication of sickness, but these can also result from a dietary change. It's best not to consider droppings' condition as a diagnosis unless the other symptoms are present as well.

If your bird is ill, and it is caged with others, it's wise to remove it to an isolated hospital cage. This will enable you to control your treatment of the disorder and keep the disease from spreading to the rest of your birds. You can convert a regular cage for this purpose by covering the back and sides with heavy cloth and heating it with a light bulb attached to the top or by a heating pad underneath. Leaving the front uncovered prevents the bird from having to spend too much time in the dark all alone. It's good for the bird's well-being for it to be able to look around the room. Since sick birds have trouble maintaining their equilibrium, place their food and water dishes on the floor and remove all the perches. You should also lower its cuttlebone so the bird can reach it easily without having to stretch.

There are a number of recognized home remedies for various diseases that may affect cockatiels. The illnesses we are going to mention here are those most often discussed by experts and the ones for which cures or treatments are well known. If you are the least bit unsure

Sick or healthy, a cockatiel should be handled with gentleness and care. This is a young, nearly-fledged chick.

regarding a particular diagnosis of your pet, consult a veterinarian. These experienced doctors should be your first source of any medical information concerning the welfare of your pet.

CUTS AND SORES

On occasion, your birds might suffer small cuts or wounds. These normally heal very quickly due to the nature of the bird's blood. To help the cure along, you should clean the wound with hydrogen peroxide and apply some antibiotic salve as often as necessary.

Your bird can develop sores on its feet if it is continually stepping in its own droppings and the feet become overly soiled.

Since the cockatiel spends every minute of its day on its feet (except when flying, of course), healthy feet are vitally important. Naturally, the best preventative for this is to keep the bottom of its cage as clean as possible, changing the paper and cleaning the perches as often as needed. However, if the feet do become encrusted, the best thing to do is to offer the bird a bath. If it refuses, as some cockatiels are prone to do, you will have to clean the feet by hand. A soft cloth and warm water will usually do the trick within a few minutes. If the condition is really bad, soak the feet in the warm water for a few minutes before wiping them clean and dry with the cloth.

A cockatiel with a broken leg can either be left alone with its normal healthy diet, or you can place a light splint made from the quill of a larger bird on the

Handle with care! Needless to say, any bird with suspect injury or illness should be handled with great care until the nature of the problem has been determined. Photo by Dr. Dr. Herbert R. Axelrod.

leg. A good diet will help it heal, but it may be crippled afterwards and unable to breed. The splint will be your best insurance against this happening as long as you make sure the toes and foot are pointed in the proper direction when setting the splint. It will take two people to do this properly, one to hold the splint in place and the other to lightly bandage the leg. Do not bandage the leg so tightly as to cut off circulation. It should only take about two weeks for a broken leg of a cockatiel to heal. As always, if you are unsure as to the proper procedure, consult your veterinarian.

A very young cockatiel afflicted with "spraddle legs." The condition is treatable. Photo by Bruce D. Lavoy.

SPRADDLE LEGS

The condition known as spraddle legs can be caused by either a parent sitting on a young chick too hard, causing its legs to spread out too far to the sides, or if the chick is on a slick surface and the weight of its own body pushes the legs out in the same manner. If you notice this condition early, you can correct it by wrapping each leg in a piece of cotton and taping the legs just above the ankle so the legs are straight enough to put the chick in a standing position. You can cut the tape to shape so it does not touch the chick's stomach. Any tape or cotton up under the chick would only become quickly soiled with droppings and slip off.

Remove the tape each day and allow the chick to exercise for an hour before rebandaging. You should see improvement in just a few days and should be able to discontinue the treatment after about a week.

BROKEN WINGS

If your bird suffers a broken wing, adhesive taping a gauze pad beneath the wing after folding it to a comfortable position against the bird's body is the best procedure. You can keep it from further damaging the wing by placing it in relatively confined quarters in a hospital cage. Many experts feel that the only thing you should do in the case of a cockatiel's breaking its wing is rush it to a veterinarian. They fear that trying to apply any kind of splint yourself could do more damage than good. The best way to prevent accidents of this nature is to make sure your bird is familiar with its flying surroundings. Don't add any new obstacles that the bird will not recognize and make certain windows of clear glass are covered so the bird will not collide with them thinking they are open space.

If, by disorientation or some other ailment or accident, your bird happens to fly into a wall, there is a good chance it may knock itself unconscious. If this happens, wrap it lightly in a soft, dry washcloth until it regains its normal composure. Then have your vet check the bird. If you haven't already done so, it might be a good idea to clip its wings. You still have to be careful even with a bird with clipped wings.

SHOCK

If your bird stands seemingly lifeless on its perch or on the cage bottom it may be suffering from shock. This can be caused by any number of things, depending on your bird's personality. Any situation that is stressful to the bird can send it into a state of shock. It might be something as serious as the aforementioned collision with a wall or something as minor as a sudden change in temperature. Whatever the reason, it must be treated within the first two days. Any further continuance of the stress could lead to the bird's untimely death.

If your bird is in a state of shock, you should keep it isolated and warm. Since heat is the best remedy for this condition, you can set your heating pad to as high as 85° to 95° F. The bird should come out of shock within a day's time. If not, consult your veterinarian immediately.

MITES

If your bird spends a large amount of time scratching, it may be suffering from mites. You can often detect these crawling on the bird's feathers. They are most often found in the nooks and crannies of the wood of aviaries. They feed on the birds' blood. There are different types of these pests and they should be eliminated as soon as possible after detection. Red mites are the kind most often associated with the cockatiel. They are actually gray in color, but after ingesting the bird's blood, their color becomes red. They are relatively hard to detect since they only attack the birds at night when the lights are off. If the bird's scratching leads you to suspect mites, cover its cage with a light cloth, wait a few hours, then quickly uncover the cage. You'll catch the pests unawares and should be able to see the little specks of gray and red on the underside of the cloth. There are a number of good commercial mite sprays found in your local pet shop.

The same holds true for the various types of lice that will, on occasion, be

Houseplants, such as this decorative but poisonous poinsettia, are among the household hazards that should be kept out of the reach of pet cockatiels.

found on cockatiels. Mites, bacteria, worms, and other pests can do a great deal of damage to your birds if they are allowed to spread. While mites can be controlled by commercial mite sprays, it's usually a good practice for the entire cage or aviary to be disinfected whenever such parasites show up. Cages should be soaked in a hot bath with a solution of disinfectant, scrubbed thoroughly, rinsed, and sun-dried. All food and water dishes, perches, and toys should receive the same treatment. You should do this once a week for three or four weeks and continue with the spray on the cage and perches.

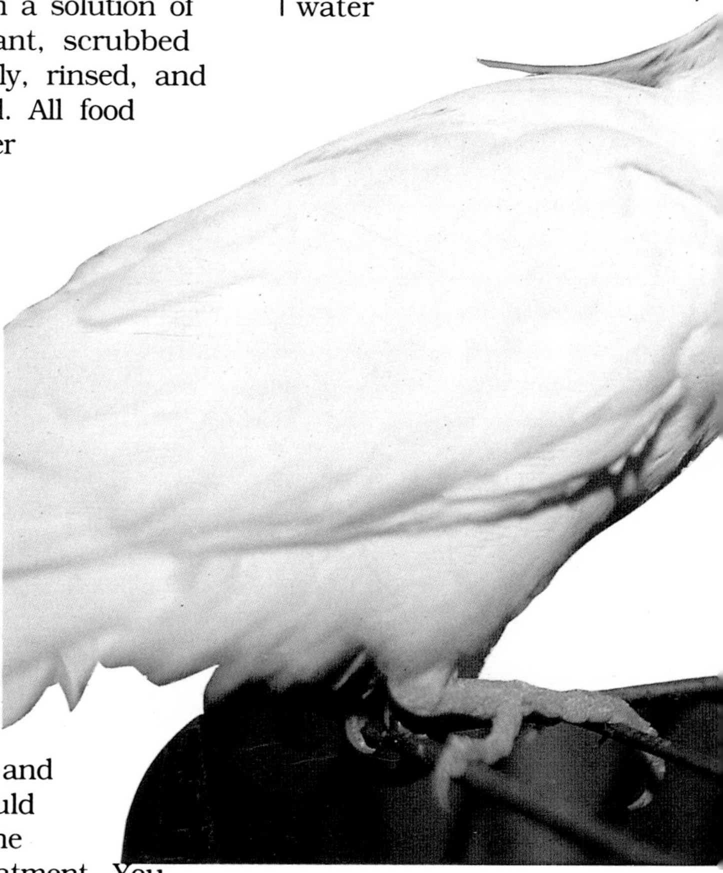

By having your birds wormed in the spring and fall, you can save them from being destroyed by these pests whose eggs are transmitted from the excreta of wild birds or, in some cases, newer birds introduced to the flock. To treat this, all green food, fruit, and water should be removed from the birds' reach for about two days. Then the anthelminthic is mixed with drinking water and given to the birds. If your bird is sick and listless, it is always a better idea to hand-feed it its medication rather than trusting it to fend for itself from its drinking water. All medication for your birds can be obtained at your pet shop or veterinarian. It is not a good idea to administer any medication without first consulting your veterinarian.

Not having had any moisture for such a long period of time, they will be anxious to take their medicine. Another method calls for injecting the mixture directly into a bird's esophagus. The dead worms will appear in the birds' droppings shortly after the anthelminthic is administered.

When your birds are free-flying in your home, be sure to watch that they do not have access to such things as your leftover food, newspapers, wallpaper, house plants or plastic bags. Ingestion of any of these can cause inflammations of the stomach and intestines. In the case of the plastic, the birds might even suffocate from eating bits of this dangerous material.

A pair of lutino pearl cockatiels engages in a little mutual preening activity. Photo by Michael Gilroy.

A bird's resistance is very low during molting, but a healthy diet should protect your bird from any

A cockatiel reflects on its relection in a mirror. As might be suspected, room mirrors can be a great hazard to free-flying cockatiels. They should be covered when your pet is given freedom to fly about.

disease during these periods.

If vomiting occurs, it is probably due to an improper diet. Change the bird's diet immediately.

DIARRHEA

While diarrhea is often a symptom of other illnesses, it is normally a result of an improper diet as well. The condition can also result from the birds' eating spoiled food or water. Vitamin B_{12} is often used successfully as a treatment. You should administer it to the affected bird while it is in isolation in a hospital cage, adding four drops to each ounce of water.

SOUR CROP

Undigested food in a cockatiel's crop leads to the condition known as sour crop. Fungus will grow and will breed infection. Sour crop is detected by the bulging of the crop and an unusual odor. To correct this, hold the bird belly up and, gently with finger pressure, work the food up the bird's neck. In this position, the food will not be allowed to enter the bird's lungs. Using a syringe with a narrow tube, flush out the crop with warm water and about $^{1}/_{4}$ teaspoon of bicarbonate of soda. Repeat two or three times. If you've detected this too late, antibiotics

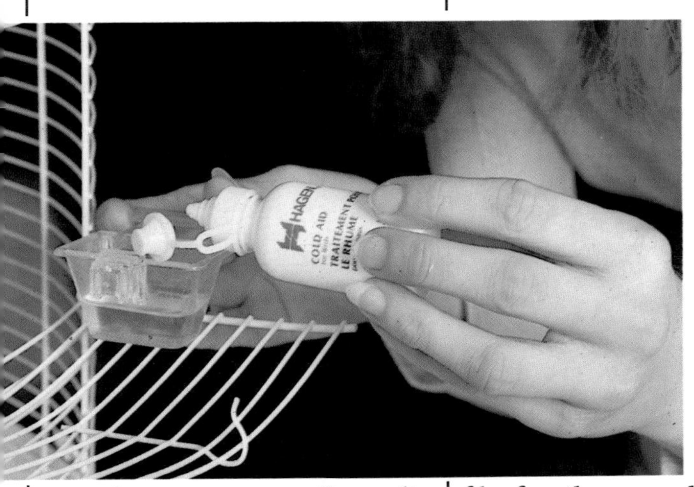

may be necessary. Consult your veterinarian if any additional problems arise.

FEATHER PLUCKING

Feather plucking in some birds is a pathological disorder, the reasons for which are not clearly known. Some experts feel it is due to a lack of mineral content in their diet. It occurs more often with birds housed alone. These cockatiels will pull out individual feathers, chew on them, and then pull another until bald patches appear. These areas often become inflamed since any new feathers are pulled out as well. Some favorable results against this disorder have been reported by adding fruit tree branches in the cage for the bird to chew on and feeding the bird a solution of sodium chloride.

Claws and upper mandibles that have grown too long can be trimmed. A nail clipper, dog toenail clippers, or scissors can be used on the claws, and a nail file for the mandible. The blood vessel of the claw is easily seen, and care must be taken not to cut into it. Trim only a small portion at a time. If bleeding does occur it will stop after a very short time and you can treat the wound with hydrogen peroxide. Clipping the claws is probably the better method since it is quicker and many birds object to the noise and feeling of a file or emery board. Filing also takes up quite a bit of time and the bird may come to associate you with this unpleasant activity. This will undo much of the positive finger training you've worked so hard to achieve.

When filing the

Remedies for some common cockatiel ailments are available at pet shops. Photo by Isabelle Francais.

The "unflappable" cockatiel? This bird is in the process of hand-taming and is being steadied and calmed by its owner. Photo by Michel Gilroy.

mandible, rub it down first with cooking oil and hold the bird's head between the thumb and index finger so the bird will not be able to bite. It may be easier to manage if a twig is inserted between the mandibles so the bird will bite on it instead of your finger. If the Cockatiel has been provided with a cuttlebone, it usually does not need to have its beak filed since its normal action with the cuttlebone grinds it down to size.

THE COMMON COLD

The Cockatiel suffering from the common cold can be treated by placing it in a warm hospital cage and adding antibiotics to its drinking water. Cold symptoms are often the same as those for some of the more serious diseases. The common cold will make your bird listless. The other symptoms are very similar to those of human suffering with a cold: they have runny noses, they refuse to eat and they will sneeze and have difficulty breathing. You may have to clear caked mucus from its nostrils with warm water and cotton or an inhalant, which can be found in your local pet shop. If your bird fails to recover after a few days, take it to your veterinarian.

If your bird has watery eyes or keeps them shut for long periods of time and then blinks them rapidly, it may be suffering from conjunctivitis. Isolating it in a hospital cage and treating the eyes with chloramphenicol eye ointment will probably clear the condition up in short order.

FRENCH MOLT

French Molt is a condition wherein the feathers on the tail and the wings are continually shedding, preventing the bird from flying properly. This condition also makes the birds look shabby. Birds who are suffering from French Molt generally have a shorter-than-average lifespan. What causes this condition is not known, but some success in preventing it has been reported by dipping the birds in a disinfectant solution to aid in preventing infection and aid in normal regrowth of the missing feathers.

We have discussed egg-binding, but it is a serious enough condition to mention here once again. The condition occurs when the hen cannot expel an egg naturally from her cloaca or lower oviduct. Birds raised on a healthy diet and who have had a good supply of cuttlebone and grit usually do not suffer from egg-binding. If the egg remains, it will block the passage of waste and the hen will die from toxemia. The cloaca can be successfully lubricated with a few drops of lukewarm water if the condition is discovered in time. Vegetable or mineral oil can also be administered instead of the water. You will probably need two people for this operation, one to hold the bird belly-up while the other lubricates the vent with an eyedropper. Afterwards, the bird

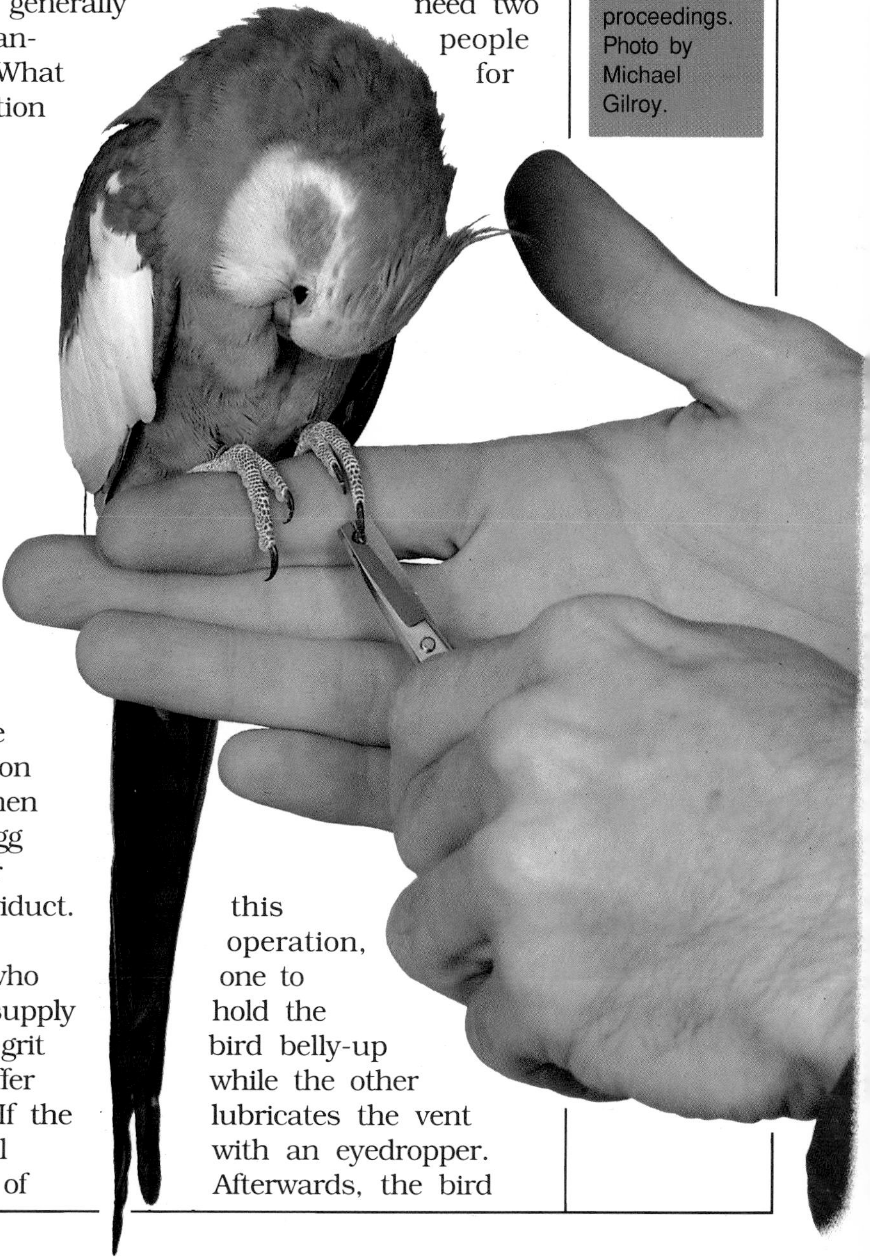

Claws should be trimmed on a regular basis. This bird seems to be keeping a close eye on the proceedings. Photo by Michael Gilroy.

The rougher, more natural the perch, the better for the bird's feet. When possible, use natural branches as cage perches. Photo by I. Francais.

can be placed in your warmed hospital cage and she will lay her egg in a matter of hours, if not sooner. She might need the aid of *slight* pressure from your fingers to pass her egg. Do this holding her belly-up again. Find the upper end of the egg and force it gently down to the oviduct toward her vent.

As we have suggested, your caged birds like fresh air at times and owners often hang their cages out of doors on a regular basis. One of the dangers of these outings can be heat stroke. Be sure you examine the cage often to make sure it is not exposed to too much direct sunlight. This could cause heat stroke. If it happens, spray your bird with cool water or wrap it lightly in a moist cloth until its temperature returns to normal.

If you detect a yellowish lump under the skin of your bird, it may have developed a tumor. If it is cancerous, it could prove fatal. Some of the superficial tumors can be successfully removed by a veterinarian. If you suspect your cockatiel is suffering from such a condition, you must take it to a vet. There is no home treatment for such a condition.

PSITTACOSIS

The parrot and parakeet disease most feared by aviculturists is psittacosis or ornithosis. This disease can be transmitted to man and has resulted in death. In some areas of the world, the birds must be tested for this disease before they can be added to a flock or bred. It usually appears in large, uncontrolled flocks of birds. The disease does not present a clinical picture, and only birds suffering a very severe infection show the symptoms of diarrhea, sleepiness, and pneumonia. In humans, the symptoms are similar to the flu.

If a large number of birds have died in your aviary, have a feces sample examined by a veterinarian or other expert to see if psittacosis has struck your birds.

The best defense against the onslaught of disease is cleanliness. Daily cleanings of the cage bottom or aviary floor as well as scheduled disinfecting of their surroundings will keep your birds healthy.

The joys of owning and caring for your own cockatiels will continue for years to come. The daily discoveries you will make by observing their activity will amaze and delight you. Many cockatiel keepers enhance these pleasures by sharing their experiences with others. Your local pet shop owner or your veterinarian will probably be able to tell you if there is a local bird club in your community.

Just as the number of cockatiel owners is increasing each year, so are the formations of such clubs. The larger and more organized clubs often have regularly scheduled meetings where bird experts and breeders come as guest speakers. The members meet to discuss and exchange ideas on the care, breeding, and raising of their birds.

Anyone who has decided to house a cockatiel, or any pet for that matter, has given a portion of himself to another living creature. The mutual trust and delight from such an association can only serve to enrich the lives of all concerned, be they human, beast, or bird.

Index